Don't

Mean

Nothing

Don't Mean Nothing

SHORT STORIES OF VIET NAM

by Susan O'Neill

SERVING HOUSE BOOKS

To Merlin:

You offered me a cigarette behind the schoolhouse when I was in third grade. If I'd have known how things were going to turn out, hell— I'd have taken it.

Susan O'Neill spent a year as an Army nurse in Viet Nam during the war. This is her first book. She has published short fiction and non-fiction in an eclectic variety of magazines, newspapers, anthologies, internet and audio media, and co-edits *Vestal Review*, a literary magazine for "Flash" fiction. She lives in Brooklyn. Her website is http://susanoneill.us .

Thanks

There are many people to whom I owe mention—and a huge debt of gratitude—for helping to make this collection the idiosyncratic little volume that it is.

First, of course, there's my patient, long-suffering husband Paul, who not only had to put up with my preoccupation, late or absent dinners, and general crankiness, but who also provided a couple of my best "bits." This, from a man who really doesn't like fiction.

There are my fellow writers on Zoetrope.com, Francis Ford Coppola's online fiction workshop, who let me know that someone might actually want to read this stuff.

And there are my kids—Kym, Kramer and Kel—who served as constructive critics and cheerleaders. My sister Diane, who really should be an editor. Jack Neary, the Vermont nurse anesthetist I've never formally met, but without whom H. Persey Jewett III would be all thumbs. Eileen Hotaling and Nancy Jones Johnson, the two Viet Nam nurse vets who together made the cover art possible (That's Nancy on the cover, snapped by Eileen, back in the 'day).

There's my agent, Nat Sobel, who helped make the book coherent and sold it here and in the UK, and more recently interceded to return the rights to me. And my previous editors, Tracy Brown of Ballantine; Bill Scott-Kerr of Black Swan, and Paul Wright and Bruce Wilcox of UMass Press. And, most especially, my current team at Serving House Books, Walter Cummins and Thomas E. Kennedy.

Finally, there are all those I worked with during a year and a month in Viet Nam. You know who you are: thanks for helping me stay sane, or for driving me crazy. It was indeed a Long, Strange Trip, and although we never chose each other, you were the best companions a young, dumb, newly-minted nurselet could have desired.

Contents

PART III – CU CHI

Introduction to the Revised Edition

I once read of an artist who sneaked into museums to revise his own "finished" paintings.

It would seem that I am doing the same thing here.

However, this new edition from the fine team at Serving House Books is a return to the book's original intent.

The two "new" stories herein, "Through the Looking Glass" and "Waiting for Charlie," were part of the original manuscript I submitted to Ballantine Books back in 2000. My editor there didn't care for them. I don't blame him: they were bloated, inexpert and downright messy.

So we dropped them.

The problem was, I had intended 'Through the Looking Glass" to introduce a pivotal character, The Lieutenant. With it, the book was a sort of novel-in-stories. Published without it, the book was just a collection.

I never felt that "Charlie," on the other hand, was essential. I wrote it as a riff on Samuel Beckett's play *Waiting for Godot*, a meditation on the true nature of war, whether in the jungle or the hospital: stretches of boredom punctuated with deadly bursts of adrenaline. I had intended it to help round the overall picture I was painting.

When Ballantine returned my rights to me, I was given the chance to re-introduce both stories into the book.

But the stories were not good.

So...I sneaked into the museum and re-worked them.

I re-wrote, chopped, pared, edited, sanded, added a few strokes, erased much, rearranged... Until at last I felt they were worthy of hanging with their brethren. Or, more appropriately, sistren.

I hope you agree that they clarify and complete.

If not, please ignore the new stories and read the book as originally published.

Now, to the overall content of *Don't Mean Nothing*:

The war in Viet Nam was rife with catchphrases. You came into the country an "FNG," a Fucking New Guy, to "Win the Hearts and Minds," and survived—it was hoped—until you were "Short" enough to "DEROS" (from Date Effective for Rotation Overseas) and go back to "The World."

The key to that survival was to bear in mind that it "Don't Mean Nothing."

"Don't Mean Nothing" was an all-purpose underdog rallying cry—a sarcastic admixture of "cool," comedy, irony, agony, bitterness, frustration, resignation and despair. Work all day on a soldier who dies? Work all day on a soldier who gets sent back into battle? Get dear-Johned? Get bit by a rat? Fall off a shipping dock and snap your spine? You couldn't control it, but you could declare that it "Don't Mean Nothing." This hip, feigned indifference was the humor of the impotent, a small bunker in the real war—the war against insanity.

I served as an Army operating room nurse in Viet Nam from May of 1969 to June of 1970. I joined the Army for the money and the travel, and because I was young and dumb and had no idea what I would be getting myself into. It was one of the biggest learning experiences of my life.

I didn't write about the Viet Nam War after I got back. I was too angry, back then. I wanted to forget about it and get on with life.

I was lucky; I'd met a good man over there and fallen in love. We didn't have to explain Viet Nam to each other. We married and worked and began a family. We made friends, moved around, bought and sold homes, went to school, changed jobs, tackled the difficult, bizarre, exciting and mellowing experience of raising three kids, traveled and grew older. The war was always there; it was an integral part of who I was. I never denied my role in it, but it was a background noise in my busy life.

Gradually, life grew calmer. My work dwindled to part-time; children drifted away from home. One day, I found myself holding my newspaper at arm's length, and it hit me—I had reached the stage in life where distance makes things clearer. So at last, in middle age, I began to put Viet Nam down on paper.

That was many years ago; this is the result.

Don't Mean Nothing is divided into three parts, one for each of the hospitals to which I was assigned during my year in Viet Nam.

There have been many novels, memoirs and short stories published about Viet Nam in the past 40 years. Most were written by men. *Don't Mean Nothing* has little in common with these, because hospital personnel—and female veterans in particular—served in a war that was substantially different from the one fought by male soldiers.

To begin with, the goal of "our" war, though considered supportive to "theirs," actually contradicted it. Soldiers were trained, and expected, to kill the enemy. We were trained, and expected, to save anyone who came through the hospital doors, which often included the enemy.

They lived with the guilt of killing; we, with the guilt of surviving. They lived surrounded by blood and death in which they had a direct stake; we faced a daily onslaught of maimed and dying men, women and children dropped on us by helicopter from an alien world. Unlike soldiers, we lived in relative comfort. We had showers—the water was often cold, but usually clean. We had some measure of privacy. We had bunks with mattresses. We had access to telephones. We had bars. We had movies. We even had television, such as it was. Soldiers seldom enjoyed these luxuries until they hit base camp.

But by far the biggest, most dynamic difference between males and females, regardless of rank and job description, was sex. Men lacked it, craved it, sometimes paid for it. Women were inundated with it, whether we wanted it or not.

The government doesn't have hard figures for how many women it sent to Viet Nam, but trust me: we were vastly outnumbered by men, and it defined us and governed our existence. We could have been ugly as toads; we could have dragged our knuckles in the dust and picked our noses in public. It wouldn't have mattered. We were pulled by demand into a vast sea of men. Embraced, seduced, conquered, sometimes impregnated and, now and then, wed.

This seemingly delightful situation had a dark underbelly. Many of us were betrayed; some, raped and abused. Some of us, too, did our own share of betraying and abusing. Revered as goddesses, madonnas and sisters, or denounced as whores, we were none of these. We were mere humans. Most of us were young and naïve, rocked by adolescent hormones, ill-equipped to play Eve to a thousand Adams.

And so, my stories are about men and women, mere human beings, living in a surreal world.

There is a base of reality: Phu Bai, Chu Lai and Cu Chi are real places, and the hospitals there were real.

Phu Bai, in the northern rolling hills between the Demilitarized Zone and the Navy stronghold of Da Nang, was a suburb of Hue, the old French capital. The inflatable MUST (Mobile Units, Self-Transporting) Quonsets of the 22nd Surgical Hospital sat atop an old Buddhist cemetery. It was a small facility, but busy. The weather was balmy-hot, the land prone to winter monsoon floods. Poison-skinned toads the size of New Jersey hung out in the latrines. Hue had been Ground Zero in the Tet Offensive of 1968; when I arrived in Spring of 1969, the staff of the 22nd were still wary of winter holidays.

The 27th Surg at Chu Lai and the 12th Evac at Cu Chi were both large metal and concrete Quonsets. Beyond that, they were vastly different.

The 27th was one of two hospitals on a huge military base filled with Marines, air support, and the Americal Division, infamous for their role in the My Lai Massacre. Chu Lai was south of Phu Bai, mid-coast, and the hospital was a short jeep ride from the headlands and white sand beaches of the South China Sea. I arrived in Fall 1969, when the US military was "Vietnamizing the War," training the ARVN (South Vietnamese army) to take their place. The hospital's load was relatively light, a high percentage of its casualties Vietnamese. We had time to swim and surf—and the "brass" also had time to insist we salute and starch our fatigues.

In Cu Chi, on the other hand, "strack" militarism was rare. The 12th Evac sat on a flat plain that once boasted peanut and rubber plantations. These had been defoliated, burned and plowed under long before I arrived in November 1969, but helicopter-sized bugs remained, adapting happily to our shower rooms and hooches. The staff comradery was high, as was the flow of casualties from the jungled woods nearby. Later, we discovered that those woods hid entrances to a complex of tunnels that stretched from Saigon to the Cambodian border. A whole city lay beneath the Cu Chi compound, and we never knew it. A city with a hospital; perhaps they operated with our cast-off instruments.

So yes, the settings were real. What I wrote about them, however, is pure fiction. As are my characters, every one of them, right down to the monkey. People who write fiction are just grown-ups with imaginary friends; these are some of mine. The late Kurt Vonnegut put it perfectly in his marvelous "Book of Bokonon" (from the novel *Cat's Cradle*, 1963): "All of these true things I am about to tell you are shameless lies."

Between the time I began this book and the time I finished it, my husband and I revisited Viet Nam on bike. We found ourselves, one day, in a vast temple built to memorialize the North Vietnamese Army and Viet Cong soldiers who had died in the preceding fifty years, a period that encompassed both the French occupation and what the Vietnamese rightfully call the "American War."

The inside of the building was lined with marble plaques, on which were engraved the names of our enemies and their dates of birth and death. There were men and women; there were many children—14, 15, 16 years of age.

This memorial only represented the VC and NVA who had been killed. There were no names of ARVN soldiers or Montagnards who had died fighting on our side. Nor were the many who had died after the war in "re-education" camps listed.

Even so, there were more than a million names. This, in a country roughly the size of New Mexico.

When we came out of the temple, we saw ragged little kids darting about in the sunshine and young couples strolling through neatly-kept meditation gardens. Tourists snapped pictures. Groundskeepers tidied flower beds. In spite of all the loss, in spite of the furor, the defoliation of land, the human and animal deformities from residual chemicals, the social and economic ostracism of pro-American soldiers—in spite of all this, life went on.

Viet Nam is still, in large part, a poor country of rice paddy farms and sandy harbors, where fishermen cast nets from boats with eyes painted on the bows. It is overcrowded, prey to floods and sweatshops and impossible traffic, dotted by modern cities and tiny hamlets of thatched huts with TV antennae. It is not a great capital of industry, nor an international oil field, nor a world-class bread basket. Although the US takes advantage now of its low-cost labor, there is really nothing in Viet Nam at present that we would find worthy of a war. And there was even less back in the 1960s. This country, these people, posed no real threat to us. It was a strange place to send our youth, not to learn a new culture or enjoy the beaches, but to kill and be killed, to be maimed and to patch up the maimed.

What I'm saying is, to us as a country, Viet Nam truly *didn't mean nothing.* And yet, look at what we did, and the damage, both here and there, that it wrought.

I wish that, by writing this little book of mine, I could make people understand that war accomplishes nothing positive. I wish I could change the world, and make it a place where no one would have to lose a child because their government decides to further its immediate political goals by killing people. But, of course, I can do none of this. I'm not that brilliant, that insightful, that strong.

All I can hope to do is to set these true and shameless lies in front of my readers. To entertain them; to make them think; to tell them that, for me, this—the tragedy, the irony, the death, the sex, drugs, rock-and-roll and, yes, that gallows humor peculiar to survival in war—is just a bit of what the Viet Nam war *did* mean.

Susan O'Neill

Don't

Mean

Nothing

PART I

Phu Bai

Through the Looking Glass

The plane drops into the stygian night, and the Lieutenant tells herself: *You have sold your soul for Irony.*

The thought is faintly depressing. It is also in itself somewhat ironic. Now, in her twenty-first year, the Lieutenant is reading Nietzsche, and has decided that she doesn't own a soul.

A bump. The plane races over an uneven runway. She closes her paperback copy of *Thus Spake Zarathustra*. Her eyes are glazed behind smudged glasses. She has the ghost of a headache; her armpits are sour, her hair rank; her tongue coated with slime. She bumps her nose against the window and sees nothing but darkness. Not even runway lights.

"Toto," the Lieutenant says under her breath, "we're not in Kansas anymore."

The guy next to her, a big PFC, a stranger to whom she's been welded from armrest to shoulder for the past twenty-four hours, opens his eyes.

"We're here," she says.

"Huh? Where?"

She nods toward her dark window. "Paradise."

"Oh, fuck," he says.

Waiting is a military specialty. At Fort Sam Houston, Texas, the Lieutenant waited in line for housing, supplies, meals, inspections, transportation, immunizations, medical attention, the latrine and, once, to slice a hole in the trachea of a goat. It had been a hands-on demonstration of a life-saving emergency procedure, a cricothyroidotomy, and there had been six nurses to one animal. The goat, its life saved six times over, had died because it couldn't breathe through a windpipe perforated like a piccolo.

Now she waits in the sweaty darkness with the others, on the airless tarmac, beneath the airplane's metal breast. She grips the handle of her plastic overnight case in one hand, rubs a mosquito bite on her thigh with the other.

Minutes or hours pass.

Olive-drab school buses, lit only by parking lights, grind up to them. One by one, the soldiers dribble into them, filling them completely.

The Lieutenant is on the last bus. She has a window seat. The window is stuck at half-mast. She pushes her nose close to the pane and sucks at the unmoving, petroleum-flavored air.

The Lieutenant is a little claustrophobic. The temperature in the already hot bus rises. The bus driver turns the engine and the parking lights off.

The itch moves from her mosquito-bitten left thigh and expands to her trunk; it tickles up her neck and into her scalp.

Profound darkness buries the runway and the buses.

"Can't turn on the lights, man," a guy three seats back tells someone. "Charlie'll blow us to bits."

Millions of tiny spiders step smartly across the Lieutenant's flesh.

She scratches surreptitiously, then openly. It does no good. She slaps at her thigh, trying to not jostle the large Spec 3 beside her. He has dozed off, his face turned toward her, his breath fetid. She rakes her fingers through her hair and digs at her scalp. Her crotch squirms with unseen beasties. The bottoms of her feet crawl, the backs of her knees sweat.

There is no air.

The Lieutenant's heart raps madly at her ribs; she stifles a groan. She wants to touch and rub at herself to calm her body. She wants to stand; she wants to walk. To run.

But she is trapped between the metal bus wall with its useless half-agape window and the large Spec 3, who snores softly. Trapped in this wheeled sardine-can, on this airless oven runway, with the reek of strangers and the invisible jigging million-legged creatures and the blacker shadows beyond and the weirdness and the threat of dying young and stupid with the flicker of a headlight.

A tear rolls down her cheek. She slumps against the cracked cushion of the hard school bus seat, sweats, pants, sucks at the stale air.

There is absolutely nothing she can do.

And then, something lets go.

It is not orgasmic; it is an effortless glide into the great and pure peace of submission.

The Lieutenant blinks. Her muscles release; the spiders evaporate. The air stirs ever so slightly. Her heartbeat slows. She closes her eyes and breathes easily, gratefully.

This is what it's like to know that you are going to die, and that there is absolutely nothing you can do.

Away beyond the darkness and the deeper shadows of the jungle, the very first light of dawn fingers the sky. The bus grumbles to life and grinds slowly forward.

The sun beats down on a narrow road crammed with jeeps, deuce-and-a-half trucks and three-wheeled Lambrettas full of tiny, dark people. Their arms clutch chickens and children; their black eyes stare. Wary. Full of secrets.

Two days ago, the Lieutenant zipped down a California highway in a friend's Malibu convertible.

Now, this green-painted school bus. Here.

There is nothing here she knows.

Everything is new.

She rubs her eyes beneath her glasses.

It is new because it is ancient. Medieval. *Here there be dragons.*

Monstrous beasts muscle through fields, children perched like skinny birds on their backs. The dirt is an orange-red she has seen only in a crayon box. Miniature old men and women in black pajamas and straw cone-shaped hats pad by barefoot, shouldering mountainous loads, bundles, buckets, small animals. No one looks up.

Nothing in the Midwest is old.

The Lieutenant hadn't intended to join the Army, back when she was a student in the Midwest. She had worked for the McCarthy campaign, had *Come Clean for Gene.* She'd met the recruiter, a fat sergeant, at a great-aunt's dinner party on a visit to Chicago. *Come to my office*, he told her. He told her the Army would pay her for her last year as a student.

The not-yet-Lieutenant was broke; she was about to leave nursing school because she couldn't pay for her final year. "I don't want to go to Viet Nam," she told him flatly. "I might be poor, but I have my principals."

He had laughed. "There's a waiting list a mile long of nurses who want to go to Viet Nam. You won't go," he said. "You *can't* go. Trust me."

The not-yet-Lieutenant considered this. *It's only two years. A person can do anything for two years.*

A dump truck full of soldiers passes the bus. The men catch sight of the Lieutenant through the window and elbow each other and wave. The Lieutenant ignores them.

A teenaged girl wobbles down a dirt path on a bike. She wears a long white dress split to the waist on both sides to show black trousers. Tied to her bike's rear fender is a wire cage filled with live piglets.

The Lieutenant was the only child in her lower-middle-class family who hadn't grabbed her high school diploma and run straight to a factory job. She was the only Atheist in her Catholic nursing school, the only student who read Yung. The only one who had marched against the war.

She was the sole girl in the family. Her mother was dead of breast cancer; her two brothers had, with Doc Hennecker's help, discovered medical conditions that made them unsuitable for military service.

She had, yes, always relished irony.

She watches two young men walk along the roadside holding hands. She takes off her glasses and polishes the lenses with the damp skirt of her uniform.

The day after the party, the Lieutenant filled out a raft of forms in triplicate, submitted to a physical exam to prove she could breathe without a respirator, and swore she wasn't a Communist. She left the recruiter's office and called home from a pay phone.

Her father answered.

"I just joined the Army," she told him.

The line went silent.

She thought they had been disconnected, and was about to hang up when he said: *Well. I guess you know what you're doing.*

The bus bumps past three old women in a flooded field who pull clumps of spiky green plants out of the water. A fourth woman squats on the dirt dam, pants off, facing the road. Peeing.

On the first day of orientation at Fort Sam Houston's Officers' Basic school, a fat sergeant who looked very much like her Chicago recruiter announced to the sea of new lieutenants in the auditorium that there was no longer a waiting list a mile long for nurses who wanted to go to Viet Nam. *All of you*, he told them, *will get there: some sooner, and some later.*

The Lieutenant had said, "Oh, fuck."

The bus passes a half-dozen stick-and-thatch houses and one stucco building with a huge hand-painted sign depicting a nude woman drinking a cocktail. *Venus Bar*, the sign says.

The Lieutenant had assessed her medical talents. She was a Midwestern specialist: She could trim the horny toenails of old farmers with diabetes; she could help birth big, corn-fed babies; she could operate a little machine to aerate the lungs of fifty-year-olds with emphysema, and feed stock-car race losers through their wired jaws. She was good with cancer, TB, asthma, and bed sores.

She knew absolutely nothing that would be of use in Viet Nam.

She signed up that very first day, after orientation, for a course in Operating Room Nursing, a critical specialty that wouldn't add time to her sentence. She wasn't fond of the Operating Room because she didn't like being told what to do. But in this case, she had no idea what to do, so it seemed appropriate.

A person could do anything for two years.

Upon graduation, she received her orders for Viet Nam.

The bus shudders to a halt. The Lieutenant squints out the window at a row of long, low-slung white huts, pragmatic structures with straight American lines. A soldier standing next to the driver consults a clipboard. He calls her name.

She squeezes down the aisle with her overnight case and steps down into hard sunlight. Someone pulls her duffel and suitcase from the belly of the bus and sets them in the roadside dust.

The bus pulls away.

A young sergeant with a thin, dark mustache riffles through a sheaf of papers. "Looks like you're going to Phu Bai. Twenty-second Surg." He winks at her meaningfully. "Phu Bai," he says, "is All Right."

"Phu Bai is All Right," she says.

She wonders what that means.

"That's one of our Magic Inflatable Hospitals." He grins and hands her a form. "Won't have to worry about getting bored up there, Lieutenant. But watch the toads in the latrine."

"Toads."

"Yeah. They got these toads up there, their skin oozes poison shit. Got a buddy up there, told me about it. Name of Scully. He's a clerk, too."

She nods. "Scully."

"Get to know him, Lieutenant. Not to be immodest, but clerks are God in this man's Army."

"Clerks."

The sergeant summons a squat, muscle-bound Spec 4 to show the Lieutenant to the Temporary Quarters.

The Temporary Quarters is a bare-bones dormitory, two long joined rooms lined with narrow cots. The Lieutenant moves to the rear of the second room. She is the only person in the place. She strips off her uniform and digs fatigues out of her duffel. The clean pants and T-shirt feel cool for a moment against her gritty skin, then warm and wilt and stick to her body. She sets her glasses on the bedside table, drops onto the narrow cot and drifts immediately to sleep.

Minutes or hours later, the Lieutenant flails awake from a dream of drowning.

"Oh, goodness." The voice is high-pitched, deep-South. "I'm sorry—Did I wake you? I'm *so* sorry. Goodness."

The Lieutenant gropes for her glasses, crams them on. She sits up, panic ebbing to disorientation.

"I'm so clumsy. Just my big old suitcase fell over—see? Nothing broken." The woman is tall and raw-boned, in full army uniform. She is slightly older than the Lieutenant, and her flat soda-jerk hat bears polished double silver captain's bars. Her perfume smells of wilted orange blossoms. Her smile is big and sheepish. "I hope I didn't wake you?" *Ah* hope. *Ah* didn't.

Her earnestness cuts through the fog. "I think I woke my—"

"Oh—thank *heavens*!" The Captain plops onto the next cot. She is Captain Amy DuCharme from North Carolina. "I am *so* excited," she says. "They're sending me up into the Central Highlands—I'm going to be *right* near my husband. He's a supply sergeant in the Cav." She blushes lantern-red. "We just got married."

The Lieutenant yawns. "I'm going to Phu—"

"I requested the posting specifically," Captain Amy DuCharme says. "In point of fact, I joined the Army *specifically* to be with Walter." Her raw, red face radiates New Love; her long white teeth dazzle.

The Lieutenant nods, feeling surreal.

"Do you know what they call us-all?"

The Lieutenant shakes her head. "Who—" "Us *new* people here?" Captain Amy DuCharme lowers her voice to a conspiratorial stage whisper, although there is no one else to hear. "They call us-all FNGs." She blushes even redder; the Lieutenant is astounded that it's possible.

"FN—"

"It means," the Captain whispers, "Eff-ing New Guys."

The Lieutenant ponders this.

"You know, I was kind of afraid to join up at first," the Captain says, "But then I thought, it's the United States *Army*, right? I'll be in a hospital, right? There's all those *men* out there to protect us-all. You know," she leans closer, "There hasn't been a woman died yet in this war."

The Lieutenant must look a bit dubious, because Captain Amy DuCharme puts her hand over her heart. "Honest. My *recruiter* told me."

The Lieutenant nods. Orange blossoms tickle her nose; she stifles a sneeze.

The Captain removes her soda jerk hat and fans herself with it. "You know, it's just so *hot* here, it's just tuckered me out. I could just drop right here," she says, "but I think I'm going to leave you in peace and take a cot down yonder." She grabs the Lieutenant and gives her a bear-hug. "It's been *so* nice talking to you. I'll always remember you as the *very first* fellow nurse I met in Viet Nam."

The Lieutenant feels crushed and orange-sticky, and is glad when the Captain releases her.

"Wish me luck!" Captain Amy DuCharme winks.

"Good l—"

"And you, have yourself the *best* of luck."

Captain Amy DuCharme marches off to the front room. The Lieutenant sighs, pulls her glasses off, falls back on her bed, and drifts back to sleep.

Minutes or hours pass, fitful with dreams of running and falling, of Jabberwoks with eyes of flame. The Lieutenant bolts awake, her shoulder shaken by the muscle-bulked Spec 4 who led her here.

"Your ride to Phu Bai's arrived, Ma'am."

The Lieutenant splashes herself at the sink, glances in the little mirror above it. She has never looked this bad, not even the morning after her graduation bacchanal. She throws on her fatigue shirt and lugs her overnight case through the Temporary Quarters.

In the front room, Captain Amy DuCharme lies newly-wed and fragrant on the cot nearest to the door.

Late afternoon sunlight sifts through the screen, over the Captain's peaceful, peeling, freckled, sleeping face, over the thumb that is planted firmly in the Captain's mouth. Clutched tight in her fingers, against her gently working lips, is something square, soft, and bright pink.

The Lieutenant halts. She bends to take a closer look.

It is slightly smaller than a handkerchief, and its color sets it apart from the olive drab sheet at the Captain's chin.

It is a piece of fuzzy flannel edged with frayed satin, a corner from a tattered blanket.

The Boy from Montana

Smoke hung like a curtain in the dying light, softening the lines of Agnes Reedy's face. It was a worn face, square, heavy. She squinted as she took a last drag on her cigarette, dropped the spent butt and ground it out with her sneaker. Then she picked up the crushed filter and slipped it into the pocket of her blood-stained operating room scrub shift, a strange gesture of tidiness amid the stark disarray of the dirt-bound hospital compound. She leaned against the picnic table.

"I'm sorry you had to go through something like that so soon," she said. "You've been here what—two, two-and-a-half weeks? It's a hard lesson.

"Back home, you get used to people dying, but usually they're old. Cancer, heart failure. Yeah, once or twice you'll see a kid—leukemia, maybe a car accident. But it's different—

"Nothing prepares you for this.

"The fights, the losses, all the healthy, good-looking young men. It's hell. Even now, even now—with more than six months down. It's still hell.

"Let me tell you about my first time. I hope you don't mind. After what you've just been through." She smiled briefly, ruefully. "You know, I've never talked about it, really. I just feel like now, right now, it's time—I've had it in my head so long, and I've got to tell somebody about it before I go back where nobody'll understand, nobody'll want to hear."

She glanced across the compound, over the rubber quonsets, dull green touched with soft pink from the sunset. A jeep rumbled by, kicking up dust.

On the other side of the dirt road, a man in fatigues hauled on the ropes of the hospital's flagpole as a clutch of soldiers stood to attention. A twilight ritual, putting the flag to bed. Agnes watched them, her eyes dark and private. She was 25; her eyes were ancient.

"I met the boy from Montana about three weeks after I came here. He was lying on a gurney outside, like usual–" She nodded toward the O.R. unit behind her–" and he was awake, squinting up into that gawdawfully bright sun–it was the middle of the morning. I pulled his chart out from under the mattress and checked his name and where he was from. I always did that, back then, when I was new–I was always looking for someone from Iowa back then.

"The chart said Montana.

"So I said, 'Montana, huh?' I looked him over–he was good-looking, even with all that red mud all over him–blond, blue-eyed young guy. And he didn't seem to be in any pain. I said, 'I didn't know anybody lived in Montana.' Joking, trying to–you know–make him smile.

"And he did. A little smile, and he said, 'Well, *I* do.' Then he kind of nodded off to sleep.

"I wheeled him in through the air-locks, into the first operating room. Where we were today. Toby Stewart and I scooted him onto the OR table; I cut off the front of his shirt. There was this little round bullet hole on his chest, right above his left nipple. The anesthetist started his IV and gave him some sodium pent, and I soaped up his chest and started to shave him. All very textbook."

She sat down heavily on the tabletop and drew out her pack of Salems, held it out. "No? Sure?" She shook out a cigarette, slid the book of matches from the cellophane sleeve, and lit up. Waved the match out, set it beside her on the splintered wood.

"Steve was first call surgeon that day. You've seen what a good guy he is–really sweet, quiet. Polite Southern Boy. Well, he steps up to the table, takes one look at the kid, and shoves me aside with his elbow. He yells at me–'No time for prep; get me some gloves. *Now.*'

"Steve never pushes people around. And he never yells. So

when he did, it kind of jump-started the whole place. I dropped my razor and ripped open a pack of gloves for him. Toby threw a gown over himself and dumped a bunch of sterile instruments onto the back table. He gave Steve a scalpel, dropped a handful of clamps on a mayo stand, and dragged it up. Jim came in just as Steve cracked the kid's chest; I gloved him up, and he crammed retractors into the incision. You know—" She took a puff on the cigarette—"Jim was new back then, too. I don't think he'd done more than a couple of cases. He's really an orthopedic surgeon. Not that that matters—as you know by now, all the guys do just about everything here, specialties be damned."

She rolled her broad shoulders. "God, I'm beat. Where was I? Oh, yes. A nurse—Worthen, she's gone now—she ran out and came back with a cooler full of blood bags. Another tech—Reb Orcutt—he came in and helped me start IV lines wherever we could—arms and legs—and we connected them all to blood. We pulled pump cuffs over the bags, hooked them onto poles and opened the flow clamps all the way.

"That was the first time I'd ever seen a pump cuff, incidentally. I mean, who needs something like that back home, right? These were older ones than what we used today; the cloth was pretty chewed up. But they worked just the same way, like putting a blood-pressure cuff on a blood bag.

"Anyway, while I'm ripping open sponge packs, I get a look at the boy's chest. There's blood bubbling up, spilling out around the retractors, around Steve's hands. You wouldn't believe the blood, so much of it. It was just amazing.

"Besides Reb and Toby, there was a another tech in the room. He was this tall, skinny black kid, a new guy from some big city—Detroit, maybe, or Chicago. His name was Tewksbury. While the rest of us ran around, hanging blood, opening supplies, focusing lights, throwing sterile drapes on the kid's belly and shoulders—" She took a drag on the cigarette—"better late than never—Tewksbury was just standing there.

"Tewksbury considered himself a Black Panther. He wore this black beret. Even there, even in the operating room, with his scrubs and mask.

"What the heck—none of us were going to tell him not to. It wasn't our place.

"He'd only been here maybe a week, at most. We tried to get to know him, include him in everything. I mean, I was so new myself, I went out of my way to try to make him feel welcome. But he didn't want anything to do with us; he kept himself apart. He made it absolutely clear from Day One that all of us—all us whites, and the black guys, too, guys like Sam, say, who cooperated with us whites—we were all The Enemy." She lifted her hands—square, fingernails dark with blood—in a what-can-you-do gesture, trailing smoke.

"Frankly, we figured he was in Nam because some recruiting sergeant had wanted to break him. None of us wanted to give the guy the satisfaction, so we'd taken to letting Tewksbury stand in a corner where he wouldn't get in trouble, and we just kind of went on with our business as if he wasn't there."

She paused to tap her cigarette's ash on the table edge. The light was nearly gone from the sky; across the road, the flagpole stood naked and deserted.

"So." She sighed. "Tewksbury's in the room when we're working on the boy from Montana. He's just standing there in the corner, like usual, in his scrubs and mask and that black beret. But this time—Black Power be damned—we needed all the help we could get. So I pulled him up to the table and grabbed his hand—it felt just like a dead fish—and I wrapped it around the bulb to a blood-bag pump.

"We had four of the things going, like today. One on each arm and leg. We're all pumping them up like crazy, flattening those bags right out, squeezing pint after pint after pint of O-neg right into the kid's veins—Reb's running around, taking down empty bags, hooking up new ones; whenever he gets a chance to breathe, he's pumping a cuff up. I'm doing two at a time. And now, Tewksbury's working one.

38

I mean, he's really pumping that bulb, pumping up that cuff. His eyes are absolutely huge above that mask of his, like he's scared to death, but he's pumping. Really pumping.

"Together, we kept squeezing blood into the boy—and he kept leaking it right back out.

"Up at the chest, Steve's up to his elbows in blood. Literally. We still hadn't managed to get a sterile gown on him, but he had his hands wrapped around the boy's heart and he was squeezing it, trying to get it to go on its own.

"You know that little fingertip-sized hole I'd seen in the kid's chest?" She closed her eyes. "I was such a rookie. I hadn't checked his back. All I'd seen was that little entry wound; if I'd checked his back, I would've seen the exit wound, where all the damage was. But he'd been lying on his back, on a sheet, and Toby and I moved the sheet with him onto the table."

She dropped her cigarette, stood to crush it out, recovered the butt.

"So." She climbed back onto the table. "Steve's working on the kid's heart. It was completely mangled, that heart, and he's trying to make what's left of it pump blood. Squeezing it. And every time, with every squeeze, the blood just bubbles out the holes. Everything was soaked—the kid's chest, Steve and Jim, all those crumpled-up surgical drapes.

"We were all tense, all concentrated, hardly even breathing, none of us saying a word. Except Steve; he was begging the heart to beat, begging the kid to stay alive. Every now and then, he'd stop squeezing for just a second, and Jim would poke at the heart with his needle and suture, trying to sew it up. Trying to close the holes between beats. But the sutures just kept slipping out. So Jim was cursing, very quietly.

"But the rest of us, nobody was saying a word. Reb, Tewksbury and I kept pumping the blood, bag after bag. I can't speak for the boys, but I was praying to myself, praying as if our lives all depended on it. Praying, pumping.

"Reb kept Tewksbury at it—when he emptied a bag, he pulled the bulb out of his hand and pushed a new one in. Tewksbury didn't have an ounce of fat on him, and you could see these veins in his arms bulging up like ropes when he pumped. And pumped. It's like his hand's a separate thing, the only thing really alive about him. He's stuck right to the spot where I put him; sweat's pouring down his forehead under that beret. It's dropping off his nose, which is sticking out over the mask. Dripping into his eyes. But I swear to God, he didn't even blink. Only his hand—it just kept pumping. He didn't even stop between bags, when the bulb wasn't there. He just squeezed. Like a robot. Fast, hard. Really hard."

She stared at her own hand, clenched and unclenched it.

"Too hard." It was almost a whisper.

She pulled out her cigarettes again, tapped one out, held out the pack. "No? Sorry—I forgot." She lit up, inhaled deeply, blew a long plume of smoke up into the deepening night.

"I'd say we'd been working for more than an hour when Tewksbury burst his blood bag," she said. "It exploded. Blew up. Like when you smash a bag filled with air. Like a gunshot, out of nowhere. We were all so quiet, so intent, and that noise—ah, God. It's like it just blew everything—instruments, pump-bulbs, even the anesthesia stuff—right out of our hands." She glanced at the glowing tip of her cigarette; music from a distant stereo drifted by. The Stones' *Satisfaction*.

She said, "It woke us up, brought us back to our senses.

"The blood from the bag—it made this wet sound, sort of *spockled*—all at once, all over the ceiling, the walls, the floors, the lights, the instruments on the tables, Steve, Jim, all of us. It splattered on our masks. It hit our eyes and noses. Hit the corners of the room, all of them, top and bottom. All these little tiny red spots, like fine spray paint. I even found blood behind my knees when I took my shower.

"Someone—I don't even remember who—removed the bulb from Tewksbury's hand and led him out. I saw him go; his hand was still pumping."

She took a deep breath, tapped the ash off her cigarette. "I never saw Tewksbury again."

Agnes Reedy shifted her feet on the long board seat. Her sneakers were streaked with blood and dirt, but they still shone softly in the dark. Her voice, when she spoke, was low and husky. "Well, after we all started breathing again, Steve—very gently—sets the boy's heart down, back in his chest. It twitched and leaked once or twice, like it was trying to beat, then—nothing. Jim threw down his needle-holder; his last suture slipped out, just like the others. I remember how it looked, this thick red thread dangling down over the bloody sheets. I can't forget that; when I'm threading needles now, I still think about it. Funny, how some things stick in your mind." She inhaled, exhaled smoke. "Steve and Jim, they both just stepped back and pulled off their gloves, and they left. They didn't say a word.

"Worthen came in and wheeled the boy's body out. We all stood there and watched her. When the kid was gone, Toby packed up his bloody instruments and carried them off. And Reb and I were left to scrub down the room.

"It took us hours, the whole rest of the day. Neither of us said a thing; we just scrubbed the blood off the floor, the table, the walls, the light, the ceiling."

She was silent for a moment. Then she said, "When I finally came out of the OR, there was a sunset. A nice one, like tonight's. And the guys were putting the flag to bed.

"I was just standing there, watching them take the flag down, fold it up into that little triangle. Just another day. Business as usual."

She shook her head, "I looked down at all that blood on my scrub dress, and I thought about the boy from Montana. How I heard his last words—they were nothing special, nothing *profound*, but they were his last words. His *last words*, and I heard them. Not his parents or his girlfriend back home or maybe even his wife, if he had one. Me. A complete stranger.

"And I thought about Tewksbury."

She squinted as she took the last drag, then dropped the butt. "Just another day for the flag." She stood and ground out the cigarette. "Business as usual."

Agnes Reedy bent over and picked up the flattened filter. "Between you and me," she said, as she dropped it in her pocket, "I haven't saluted the flag since then."

Butch

Spec 4 August Wray met his son—the child of his heart, if not his loins—in June of 1969.

That April, the Army had sent Wray to work in the inflatable surgical hospital at Phu Bai. Although he never talked about it, Phu Bai was, for him, truly All Right: being at a hospital meant he didn't have to use a gun.

Wray had first used a gun on his tenth birthday, when his Uncle Hinton had taken him into the northern Maine woods to kill a deer. It was intended to be a rite of passage.

It was a sultry August morning—too damned hot, Hinton had joked, for the game wardens—and the two had hunkered silently behind a screen of trees and pine brush, sipping from a thermos of cold coffee sweetened with condensed milk. Shortly before noon, a small white-tailed doe stepped stiffly, gracefully, into the far end of the clearing in front of them. Wray's uncle lifted his gun from his lap, cocked the hammer almost noiselessly, and brought it to the boy's shoulder. Wray sat transfixed, staring down the long barrel at the deer, not daring to breathe. She was astonishingly close, upwind, unconcerned, cropping thick tufts of weeds.

"Now—just squeeze the trigger," Hinton whispered.

The gun kicked, shattered the peace of the forest, rattled the boy's ears. When he opened his eyes, the creature was gazing straight at him. A fat dribble of blood traced a line between her liquid brown eyes, and she buckled down into the wild grass and pine needles.

August Wray dropped the rifle and retched.

Uncle Hinton turned stiffly; his eyes traveled from Wray's scarlet face down to his favorite Winchester, which lay in a pool of vomit that was already drawing flies. "Well, you are your mother's son, may she rest in peace." He sighed. "Thank the lord, you don't need to shoot nothing to be a potato farmer."

And so, it was August Wray the potato farmer who found himself, ten years later, humping bedpans on the Medical Holding ward in Phu Bai. August Wray, who believed with a farmer's simple faith in His Country, Right or Wrong—but who also believed that, if he had to spend 365 days alone serving that country, it was better to spend it wallowing in disease, blood, pus and shit, than shooting people down like deer.

Wray was a big man who worked easily with tractors and plows, but was absolutely, irredeemably all-thumbs shy with human beings. Especially women, whose very presence could strike him dumb. He had fallen hopelessly in love with Cherry, a woman-child as sweet and round as her name, when they were freshmen in high school. She finally noticed, approved, and—when all else failed—asked him for a date. The day they graduated, she proposed.

Uncle Hinton beamed with pride on the boy he'd raised and the splendid creature he had—God only knew how—won for himself, and he gave the couple a plot of land on the farm. There, in a little modular house, they lived blessedly, happily, for a year.

On the eve of his 20th birthday, three weeks after he brought Cherry home from the hospital with their brand-new twin baby girls, August Wray got a notice from the Army.

And now, here he was. In Phu Bai.

August Wray missed his wife terribly, and thought obsessively of her blue eyes and wild red hair, and the way the skin on her bottom felt under his big, hard hands. He missed his little baby girls so much it made his eyes sting. He missed his uncle's dry grin, and the dark, cold earth of his up-country farmland.

All this missing left Wray feeling like his chest was split wide, like his heart was hanging out, huge and obscene, for all to see. So when he bent over bed 14 in the Holding Ward one hot mid-June day, all the little fellow in it had to do was reach up and touch him, and that heart was his.

* * *

They called the kid "Butch" because no one knew how to pronounce his real name. He was six, but he didn't look much bigger than August Wray's own little girls in Cherry's latest snapshots. Lt. O'Callahan had once told him that gooks started numbering ages at birth, so a newborn was already one year old. Still, whether he was six or only five, Butch was entirely too small. And too quiet. When Wray bent over bed 14, the child lay with his thumb in his mouth and his eyes wary, the sheet drawn up to his scrawny neck.

"Poor little Sprout," said Wray, shaking his head.

Lt. O'Callahan had asked Wray to change the kid's diaper.

At home, Cherry never asked him to change diapers; it was a woman's job. Here in Holding, however, when a baby was admitted to care for some medical condition before going to surgery, diapering was Wray's job. This was because Lt. O'Callahan was the only woman on his shift—and while she was on duty, she was not by Army definition a woman; she was an officer. Wray was grateful for the distinction. He could work with an officer: working with a woman, even a nurse, would have rendered him catatonic.

August Wray had attempted to change his first diaper two weeks after he'd arrived on Holding. But the baby had been too little, and his fingers had been too big; he'd accidentally stuck the pin into the poor wriggling creature's thigh.

By the time he met Butch, he was—thanks to Lt. O'Callahan's patience—an expert in the art.

In the close rubber ward, with sweat dripping off his nose because the air conditioner was no match for the heat, August Wray sat down on bed 14 and laid the diaper over his knee. He pulled the bedsheet back, and what he saw made his stomach sink. The boy's legbones were bowed in a circle, so that the soles of his feet were touching. Above them, the belly was bloated, pregnant-looking. Wray looked up into Butch's black eyes; the child looked back, sucking his thumb.

August Wray swallowed hard and unpinned the boy's diaper. The child's pelvis seemed so tiny—what with his big belly, and his legs sprouting like arches right out of it—that he wasn't sure where he could pin the clean cloth. "You got to stay real quiet, little Sprout," he said, as he brought the diaper up over the kid's tiny little wiener and tucked it down below that hard gut. The boy lay unmoving, watching Wray's eyes.

When he had finished, Wray carted the wet diaper to the hamper. He returned to bed 14 to find the boy sitting up, his hands resting atop his swollen belly. He looked like one of those little statues of Buddha that they sold in the PX, except that he wasn't smiling.

Wray sat down; Butch reached up and touched his arm.

August Wray picked the boy up.

"Watch that stuff on his back," Lt. O'Callahan said, sticking a thermometer in the mouth of the G.I. in the next bed. The G.I., a small black man from Alabama, was slated to have a circumcision because his privates had been damaged by a raging infection he'd gotten from a whore in Hue. He was in Holding because the surgeons couldn't operate until his disease was cured.

Wray avoided looking at the man because he knew too much about him. He shifted Butch on his lap and examined the child's lower back. The skin was covered with red weals.

"Leave that in, Seymour," Lt. O'Callahan told the G.I., "Or I'll have to give you the rectal one. Isn't he a mess?"

"Yes, Ma'am." Wray wondered whether she meant the G.I. or the child.

"They get that skin cleared up, Jim and Steve are going to

46

break his legs and set 'em straight." She wrinkled her freckled nose and grasped the black GI's wrist. "He's kind of got the mange. Along with malnutrition, along with rickets, along with he's an orphan." She looked down at her wristwatch. "Poor little shit."

The black G.I. spoke around the thermometer. "Guess that's one little motherfucker won't be toting a gun."

Lt. O'Callahan flicked him an ominous look. "I got a rectal thermometer with your name on it, honey."

He shut his mouth.

The boy leaned back in Wray's arms, eyed him seriously, and stuck a finger up into the man's large nostril.

"Jim says some nun found him in a bunker up in Hue after Tet last year," Lt. O'Callahan said, her eyes on her watch dial. "I guess they had him in the orphanage since then. The guys took a medcap team out to the place a couple days ago, and there he was." She pulled the thermometer out of the G.I.'s mouth and squinted at it. "Since you've got him, Auggie, why don't you see if you can't get something in him? George brought a bowl of jello from the mess tent—it's there on his table, if it hasn't melted." She shook the thermometer down with a jerk of her wrist. "One-oh-one, Seymour. You're coming down. Almost ready to get the old pencil sharpened."

The G.I. rolled over and pulled his sheet over his head.

August Wray set the boy next to him on the bed. "We're gonna eat us some jello, little Sprout." He dug into the cup of oozing green stuff and lifted a spoonful to the boy's lips. Butch pushed it aside; the jello dropped to the bed, leaving a thin smear on the white sheet.

Wray scraped it up with his spoon. He took the boy's hand, turned it palm-up, and plopped the stuff on it. Then he jiggled the little mound of green light with his own finger. Butch frowned and closed his fist, and the jello squished through his fingers.

Wray laughed aloud. The sound startled the child. It also startled Wray himself, and brought Lt. O'Callahan to the bedside.

Wray looked up at her, his smile gone sheepish.

The Lieutenant patted him on the shoulder. "Whatever it takes, Auggie," she said. "Whatever it takes."

* * *

By the first of July, Butch's belly had shrunk to child-sized and he had gained five pounds—healthy weight that plumped his face and limbs. August Wray took a modest pride in knowing that he had almost single-handedly effected this miracle. He fed the boy every day, even on his day off. He brought him precious Almond Joy candy bars Cherry sent from home, potato chips and pudding from the mess tent, pizza from the E.M. club. These things he would place on the child's palm; Butch fingered them, then crammed them into his mouth.

The boy developed a beaming, snaggle-toothed smile that pulled everyone near him into its field. Vietnamese teenagers gave him wheelchair rides. Nurses from other wards stopped in to pinch his cheeks. Corpsmen brought him small toys from the PX.

Wray routinely ate his meals alone at a corner table in the mess tent, where he could pore over Cherry's daily letters uninterrupted. One mid-July evening, George, the taciturn black corpsman who worked the night shift in Holding, sat down beside him. Wray found the meal a bit strange—silent, almost ceremonial—but surprisingly comfortable.

The very next day, Ron from Triage joined them, as did Orcutt from the OR and Harper and Nealon from Post Op. August Wray felt somewhat uneasy; he tucked his letters carefully into his pocket for later, touching them now and then during the meal to assure himself that they were there.

Days passed, and he found he had company at every meal. He buttoned his pocket flap over his letters, and tuned in to the conversations at his table. They were lively and ribald—and even as he blushed at the men's jokes, he found himself laughing.

A week later, Lt. O'Callahan took him aside to tell him that she was happy to see him working so quickly and efficiently. He colored up, then instantly reminded himself that she was an officer and not a woman. It was true; he was working faster—because when he finished washing, feeding, changing dressings, making beds, hauling bedpans, taking pulses, temperatures, blood pressures—then, he could spend a few hoarded moments with Butch. He read to the child, helped him listen to his own quick heartbeat through the stethoscope, taught him how to play pat-a-cake and peek-a-boo.

One afternoon, as he bathed a paralyzed soldier who was waiting in Holding for a transport home, August Wray found himself humming a small, wordless country air, one that Cherry had sung to pacify their babies. He halted immediately, red-faced.

"I'm sorry," he told the soldier. "Couldn't carry a tune in a bushel basket."

"That don't matter." The young man's expression was wistful. "I was just thinking how you're the first person I've heard humming since I got to 'Nam. It made me realize how much I miss stuff like that."

Very early every morning, in the quiet darkness before his shift, August Wray sat hunched on his cot, laboriously penning his daily letter to Cherry and the girls. In slow block letters, he told them about how he'd found flowers growing wild between the inflatable Quonsets and had transplanted them to a tiny patch next to his hooch. He wrote about the toads in the latrine, midnight breakfast, Liar's Dice at the club, George's girlfriend back home—random details of a life apart.

He wrote nothing about Butch.

He carried the seed of an idea in the back of his mind, but he was afraid to speak it, to write it, because it might prove too fragile for the weight of daylight.

In the night, however, he dared imagine himself in Maine.

With Butch.

Cherry fussed over the boy and declared him "cunning as a bunny." His girls, babies as he had left them, turned eager, identical blue eyes to their big brother. And Uncle Hinton announced to his late sister in heaven that this child—straight and tall—would most certainly be a Real Man.

These were not things that August Wray could write. Not yet. He was a patient man; he knew that when something needed to grow, you couldn't hurry it.

* * *

By the end of July, Wray had taught Butch a list of useful English words. *Jello*—now the boy's favorite food. *'Tenat*, for Lt. O'Callahan. *Up. Bed. Wata*, for water. *Yum*, for any food that wasn't jello. And *pee-pee*, for when he wanted the urinal. Getting him out of diapers had cost Wray nearly three whole days of concentrated effort, but he'd been rewarded by the amazement and—yes—admiration on Lt. O'Callahan's face.

He also taught Butch to call him Da-da. The first time the child had said it in the presence of Lt. O'Callahan, Wray had held his breath. But the lieutenant had said nothing—and he'd realized, with a rush of humility, that she must have thought the title appropriate.

By the end of July, the boy had lost the mange. He was walking, toddling on the outsides of his ankle-bones, grabbing for support on cots and chairs and the legs of passersby. A dozen times a day, Butch played with the metal dogtags that dangled from a chain around Wray's neck as the corpsman hunched over him, gingerly peeling blood-stuck gauze pads from his ankles. A dozen times a day, Wray piled on clean pads, wrapped the little feet with kerlix bandages, and covered them over with GI socks. And watched, his heart in his mouth, as Butch slid from the bed and hobbled away again; moving, moving, always moving.

The population at Wray's table in the mess hall exploded, because Butch now ate beside him on a chair piled with old books.

Corpsmen pulled up seats. Doctors stopped by. And nurses—nurses! Wray sometimes spent entire meals mute, dropping string beans into his lap, while the women (the officers) ogled and cooed over the boy.

Every night, without fail, August Wray tucked Butch into bed 14. He covered him, gave him a tiny peck of a kiss, and stood watch as the boy drifted to sleep, his thumb in his mouth. Then, after making sure no one else could hear, he leaned close to the boy's ear.

"Goodnight, Son," he whispered.

* * *

On August fifth, Wray nearly skipped into Holding, bearing a special treat for the boy—a Twinkie, one of a whole box Cherry had sent for his birthday gift.

He halted abruptly and gaped at bed 14.

It was full of Vietnamese peasants. Two babies slept on the pillow. An old woman sat at the foot. On the floor beneath her, two small girls squatted over an electric wok, cooking rice. The pungent odor of nuc mam hung in the air.

Wray's hand mashed the Twinkie inside its cellophane.

"It's okay, Auggie," said Lt. O'Callahan from her desk. "He's in surgery. Mina dropped by a minute ago and said they just started working on him."

Wray's heart pounded. A great and terrible fear filled his head.

What if something went wrong?

He stared down at the flattened cake in his hand.

What if it hurt? Would it hurt?

He reached out to steady himself against the wall, his legs suddenly weak.

That evening, he bore a new, uncrushed Twinkie into Post Op.

Butch lay in a stretcher bed. His face was pale as the sheets, his black eyes bleary. Wray showed him the treat. The boy turned his head away.

August Wray set the little cake on the bedside stand. Breathing hard, he advanced on the nurse's desk, and stood over the small, homely woman seated behind it. "Ma'am." He cleared his throat. "Butch—the little guy. He's in pain, Ma'am."

Cpt. Mina Griswold glanced up from a chart. "I just gave him something, Specialist." The words were crisp, and defied opposition.

Wray stuck out his jaw. "Begging your pardon, Ma'am, but—it isn't enough." He grimaced, shocked by his own boldness.

Cpt. Griswold squared her shoulders and rose. "We'll see about that, Specialist."

The big man and the tiny woman stood together at the bedside. Butch sniffled. His hands twitched.

"See?" said Wray.

Cpt. Griswold felt the boy's pulse. "He's fine. I gave him something—it hasn't had time to take effect yet." She sighed. "Look— you don't want to overmedicate somebody that small, Specialist. You'd make him sick as a dog."

He moved closer to the bed.

Cpt. Griswold placed a hand softly atop the sheet. "You can look, if you want," she said. Her voice was tired, conciliatory. "Here." She gently lifted the sheet and brought it down to the foot of the bed. Butch lay still, eyes shut.

Where the bowed legs had been, two straight white casts lay propped on a pillow. "They broke each leg once and set them," the captain said. "He's young enough, they should heal straight."

August Wray examined the row of small pink toes at the end of the casts, then carefully covered the child again.

Cpt. Griswold pulled a folding chair up to the bedside and nodded for him to sit down.

He jerked awake when the child whimpered. Butch's eyes were open, clear, and very unhappy. Wray's heart rose. *He's going to make it.*

He squinted at his watch; barely time to write his letter before work. He took his Twinkie from the stand and set it next to Butch's pillow. "For when you feel better," he said, watching the boy nod off again. He carefully touched the hard casts beneath the sheet. "Happy birthday to you, too, I guess."

* * *

"Shit. Fuck. Son of a *bitch!*" Lt. O'Callahan threw the papers down on her desk and folded her arms. "Well, it's not a rumor, damn it. I'm going to Qui Nhon."

August Wray stopped in his tracks, a full bedpan in his hands. She gave him a *look.* "Well?"

His face flushed; he lowered his eyes and made for the hopper at the end of the ward. It worried him, when the lieutenant got cranky; it worried him because it didn't used to happen very much—and lately, it seemed to happen a lot, and at the oddest times. Two mornings ago, during report, she made a curt remark about a patient. Yesterday, while taking a pulse, she suddenly began to rail about how she was *sick and tired* of eating powdered eggs and drinking filled milk.

When the lieutenant got cranky, he was apt to forget that she was an officer and not a woman. She threw him off-balance and made him clumsy; she reminded him of Cherry when she was expecting the twins—except that Lt. O'Callahan didn't throw up in the morning and crave steamed clams.

Wray stared meditatively at the turds whirlpooling down the hopper hole. He hoped it would pass, the lieutenant's mood. Quickly.

Surely, she wouldn't really go to Qui Nhon. How could the Army close down a whole hospital? It was too big, too important. What would they do with the patients?

The concept was beyond his grasp; the whole thing had to be a rumor. There were always rumors in Viet Nam—about troop cutbacks, drug crackdowns, imminent victory. George always said, *Don't believe it until you see it.* George was a smart man, and August Wray was inclined to agree with him.

He wiped the pan and glanced across the room at bed 14, where Butch sucked his thumb and stared at a Superman comic book.

They wouldn't abandon a helpless little Sprout with both of his legs in casts.

Wray carried the empty bedpan past Lt. O'Callahan, moving quietly on the balls of his feet. She was sitting at her little metal desk, her elbows on the blotter and her head in her hands, the very embodiment of Despair.

Don't believe it until you see it, he reminded himself.

* * *

August Wray saw the Surg move in early September.

Most of the staff had left for new assignments by then, but Wray had been ordered to remain, one of a dozen men whose temporary job was to deflate the giant Quonsets, remove them from their arched metal frames, and re-pack them in the closet-sized "conex containers" from which they had originally come. Crane helicopters then loaded them into giant, double-rotor chinooks, which carted them away.

The job was heavy and tedious. Wray worked automatically, his heart filled with anguish.

Two days before, he had loaded Butch into an ambulance full of children and ARVN soldiers, to be transported to the hospital in Hue. It was a Vietnamese hospital, one the Surg had "adopted," giving it outdated and surplus supplies. The surgeons and OR techs had also donated some of their days off to the place.

August Wray had heard them talk about maggots in the sterile OR packs and beds without mattresses.

Although he was not a praying man, he prayed as he worked— prayed like a true believer—that Butch would come out of the Vietnamese hospital alive. He knew that the boy had probably never been healthier.

54

They'd even had to change his casts once, because he was growing. Wray knew this—with his head. But in his heart, he felt only the cold certainty that no one was safe in a place like the Hue hospital.

And so, two days earlier, he had refused to give Butch over to the ambulance crew. They had reasoned with him calmly; then they had grown insistent. Finally, they had called in the MPs, to tell him what he *couldn't* do, and what he *had* to do, and what the Army could *make* him do.

At that, he'd clutched the boy fiercely in his arms.

Immediately, Butch had begun to wail, black eyes wild, arms wrapped tight around Wray's neck.

It was the feel of this stranglehold that had brought Wray back to earth. As a farmer and an orphan, he was a pragmatic man. Even as he buried his face in the boy's mop of black hair, he knew he had to give him up.

He could not keep the child with him; there was no way to do that.

Not now.

He forced himself to loosen his grip. And, gradually, Wray felt Butch's arms relax. He swallowed hard against the lump in his throat, sat the child down on the gurney, and wiped his bump of a nose with his big green handkerchief. He told the boy that he'd have to be good, that he would have to eat all the "yum" they gave him. He massaged the boy's narrow shoulders gently, then, very slowly, against his every instinct, lifted his hands off.

Butch hiccoughed softly, rubbed his eyes, fixed them on Wray. The naked trust in them broke the man's heart.

"Da?"

Wray pulled the long steel-bead chain with his dogtags off over his head. Carefully, he hung them around Butch's thin neck. The tags dangled to the boy's navel.

If you ever feel afraid, he told the boy, *you hold on tight to these and think of me.*

Think of Da.
I will come back for you, little Sprout.

Butch clasped the tags in one hand. He put his other thumb in his mouth.

Wray walked the gurney to the ambulance, watched the corpsmen lift the boy in and set him among the other silent occupants. He waved, putting on the face of a real man. It was a hollow act, and it did not cover the pain.

Now, August Wray sweated in the hard sun, pressing the last pockets of air from a segment of his own late Holding ward. Tomorrow, where rows of olive-drab buildings and canvas tents had stood, there would be only beaten dirt and the scattering of circular graves that had been there long before the Army had come to Phu Bai. His flowers were gone, torn apart by the wheels of Deuce-and-a-Half trucks.

Tomorrow, he would climb into a helicopter and fly to his new assignment in Long Binh. He would work. He still had seven months to go; he had to work. But the work would not be important.

What would be important was that, when he finally went home, his son would be with him. He would make it happen.

For the first time that he could ever remember, August Wray had a purpose wholly his own, a destiny that he had to shape, one that would not shape him.

* * *

The mid-day deluge dropped instantly and fully on the tile roof above August Wray. He stood in the archway at the entrance to the orphanage, wringing his olive-drab baseball cap in his big hands, watching the rain churn the dirt play yard to mud.

Wray felt excited, lost, terrified. The rain drummed away all sound. He saw no one in the compound. He wondered if he had made a wrong turn somewhere. Did children really live within these stark

56

walls?

A hand touched his shoulder, and he jumped. He turned to find an old nun, bird-tiny and brown in yards of stiff white cloth, gazing up at him with sharp black eyes.

She spoke.

He squeezed his hat, feeling foolish. "I'm sorry, Ma'am—no bick. You speak English?"

The nun inclined her head slightly.

"I'm looking for a boy. A little guy." He extended his hand at hip level, was embarrassed to see it tremble. "Maybe this big. His name is Butch."

The furrows in her brow deepened.

Wray fought panic. "Butch," he shouted over the rain.

Then he remembered: the child's name was not Butch.

The nun watched him patiently, saying nothing.

Suddenly, Wray pointed to his legs and pantomimed a big "O" with his arms. "From the hospital, Ma'am," he boomed. "Phu Bai."

The sister's eyes widened. She motioned for him to follow her.

She led him around the corner, following the shelter of the overhang. He made himself walk slowly, eyes on the grimy hem of her long white skirt, heart hammering.

The rain ceased abruptly; the yard steamed.

She led him into a large room. As Wray's eyes adjusted, he saw dozens of children squatting on the tiled floor. Mealtime—but there were no tables, no chairs. Each child held a bowl, scooping rice from it with chopsticks, eating in shared silence.

Wray examined the crowd. The children all looked alike: thin, black-haired, dressed in colored shirts.

The nun called out in a high old-woman voice. A small boy stood up.

August Wray held his breath. The child glanced at him with slight interest, then moved toward the nun. He carried his bowl, eating the last of his rice as he walked. He wore a madras shirt that was at least two sizes too large for his thin frame, and he limped slightly.

Wray heard a faint metallic clink.

Instantly, he forgot himself, opened his arms wide. "Butch!"

The boy raised his eyes and stared hard at him. Behind him, the other children looked up, chopsticks poised.

"Butch! It's Da!"

The boy dropped his chopsticks; they bounced against the tile floor. His small hand closed over dogtags that hung just above his waist. "Da," he said. It was little more than a whisper, but it filled the room.

A fresh rain rattled down on the roof above them. The man and the boy sat side-by-side in the archway on a mossy, ancient stone bench.

In the two and one-half months since Wray had let the boy go, Butch had grown taller. His cheeks had lost baby-fat, and his hair was clipped to a half-inch all over his head. Wray brushed a hand over it and grinned; it was the same style he'd worn as a kid. A buzz-cut.

He reached into his breast pocket and pulled out a small metal truck. "See this? I bought it for you in the PX. For Christmas. It's only about Thanksgiving right now, but—" Wray turned the little vehicle, spun a wheel with his big finger. "I tried to wrap it up proper, but the paper kept coming off." He handed Butch the truck, and set his baseball cap on the child's head.

Butch turned the truck over in his hands, then smiled up at him from under the cap's outsized brim.

The smile was different—Wray nearly cried when he saw that teeth had grown in. "It's a truck," he said slowly, loudly, clearly. It pained him that Butch had lost his English. Would it come back?
Butch lifted the truck, and Wray saw him as he had been, lifting a spoon, a book, a pencil. "Truck," he told the child. He touched the toy. "Truck," he said, almost begging.

Butch cocked his head. "Tuck."

Wray's heart expanded. He thought of Cherry, laying a soft hand on the boy's head.

My son; our son.

He put his arm around Butch and touched his lips to the top of the baseball cap. His throat ached. "I love you, little Sprout," he rasped. The honest, solid truth of it freed something in him; suddenly there was *lightness*—he floated above the steaming, empty play yard, sat on a cloud, swallowing balloons.

"Tuck," said Butch.

* * *

"We don't encourage this sort of thing," said the man. "Neither do the Vietnamese."

On the corner of the man's vast wooden desktop sat a foot-high ceramic Christmas tree with tiny colored lights that blinked on and off in unison. August Wray wanted to pick up the tree and bring it down on this small, well-tanned middle-aged man's head. The violence of the thought surprised and troubled him. He shifted in his seat and focused on the blinking lights.

On. Off. On. A long moment passed.

Wray cleared his throat. "What can I do, Sir?"

The man straightened a paper on his blotter. "Do. Well, you first have to prove that nobody else might want the boy. No relatives, that sort of thing."

Wray's hands clutched his hat in his lap. "How do I prove it, Sir?"

"Prove it. Well, you could write to the orphanage, I suppose, Mr. Wray. Or I suppose you could visit in person, if that suits you better." The little man drummed his fingers on the desktop.

"They don't speak English, Sir. The sisters."

"They don't. Well, don't you have interpreters at your hospital?" The man glanced at his watch.

Wray considered this.

The lights on the little tree blinked on, off.

"Be advised, of course, that this would only be the first of many steps you'd have to take to remove the child from this country—"

"If I do—"

The man shrugged. "If you prove the child is free, then we have to begin working with the Vietnamese," he said. "And that, I warn you, can be both frustrating and expensive. I hope you have the resources for this whole exercise."

Wray stared at the blinking tree and considered his assets. He sent most of his check home to Cherry, but he did keep a small stipend to buy a few things for himself. He owned a modest reel-to-reel, tapes of Boxcar Willie, Waylon Jennings and Les Paul, a box of souvenirs—shirts, dolls, and Buddha statuettes for his family. And there was a tiny savings account he had set up in case he wanted to take an R&R some day.

"How much, Sir?" he said.

"How much. Well, I can't say. Maybe hundreds of dollars. Maybe a thousand. Maybe more." He sighed. "Look, it's my job to call it as I see it. This is Vietnam, anything can happen. This orphan's a boy. Now, the fact that he's a cripple might work in your favor—you wouldn't be running off with a potential worker. A potential soldier. You can be thankful for that much. But even if you pay off all the right people, do all the right things—even then, who knows? The whole damned thing might blow up in your face. So—consider yourself advised." He stood and extended his hand, "Now—if you would. I really do have another appointment—"

August Wray rose. He reached down and shook the small, neatly-manicured hand. He didn't need an R&R. He didn't need a stereo, tapes, trinkets.

"Oh—and Merry Christmas, Mr. Wray," said the little man.

* * *

The sky was heavy with clouds, but no rain had fallen during the entire trip. August Wray took this to be a good omen. It had been a day of good omens, so far: Nealon and the other guys in the hooch had handed him a bag filled with candy bars (*Give this to your little guy for all of us, Aug*); traffic had been light on the northern highway; it hadn't rained. His heart was high; it was all he could do to keep himself from singing.

Beside him, in the passenger seat, Nguyen Thi Bich—known as Becky—stared out at the foliage, the dusty refugee camps, the tin shacks that lined the road. She was the best omen of all; he had been surprised and touched that the interpreter had volunteered to spend her day off with him here, even though she knew that he couldn't pay her. Gratitude had tied his tongue in knots; he hoped with all his heart that she understood how thankful he felt.

They had boarded the chopper to Da Nang at dawn. Now, as he pulled the borrowed Navy jeep into the yard at the orphanage, it was mid-afternoon.

He killed the engine and sat, gathering his courage. Becky glanced at him, then turned her eyes discreetly toward the gate.

It had been two long months since he'd seen his son. He wanted Butch to recognize him. Without the sister's help, this time. He squeezed his eyes shut.

God, he prayed silently, his hands gripping the steering wheel, let this be perfect.

* * *

They walk through the archway, and Wray glances at the bench where he last sat with the boy. He notes, happily, that the moss still climbs its stone back. This, too, is a good omen: *Two months is not so very long; few things change in two months.*

Gaggles of small children squat in the play yard. They glance up as the two adults approach. Wray looks them over, holds his breath, follows them with his eyes as they rise and bob and mill about like little dark chicks, so similar that their movements confuse him. *Stay in one place,* he wills them, *Please.*

"He is here?" asks Becky.

Of course he's here—but he will wait to tell her this until he actually sees the boy. Wray grips the rolled top of the paper bag full of candy bars with both hands, willing the children to stand still. *Of course. It's a big place; this isn't all the children.*

A tiny, erect figure in white sails toward them, stops suddenly, lifts a hand in recognition.

His heart beats faster. "That's the sister," says Wray. "She knows me." He grins and nods to her.

Her smile, when it comes, is slow and small, and does not reach her eyes.

The office is cool; Sister sets cups of tea in front of the man and the young Vietnamese woman. Wray's stomach turns; he cannot speak, and the nun does not. So he waits. His hand has turned the top of his paper bag to damp pulp.

At last, the nun sits down, across the table from them. She speaks to the interpreter. Words fall between the two women; they nod.

Becky says to him. "The boy—he is not here."

Wray's throat constricts. *Of course he's here.* He stares at the paper bag, pictures the candy inside it.

More words. Becky says, "Sister say, his uncle come for him."

Wray opens his mouth, closes it. It is desert dry. But his vision has gone dark; he couldn't find his cup of tea if he tried.

The nun reaches across the table, gently removes the paper bag from his grip; she takes his hand in hers. Her fingers are dry, like old paper. She speaks.

Becky hesitates. "Sister say the boy, he all good now, walk good. His uncle take him home." She frowns. "His uncle—-he is big

62

man in Hue, Sister say. Important man."

Wray closes his eyes and sees a child, buzz-cut hair. A rifle.

The nun reaches her free hand into the folds of her starched white habit. There is a faint metallic clink.

Wray jerks his hand free and covers his ears. The world stops, freezes.

eyes liquid brown, legs buckling.

He feels the interpreter's arms around him, holding him, but he sits still and does not react. He feels the side of her face against his cheek, but it is not until much later that he will remember it, that it was wet. Over her silk-covered shoulder he sees, now—and again and again—days, months, years from now: the nun, wizened and brown in her starched white habit, dogtags on a steel-ball chain coiled in her palm. Her eyes knowing, her face pinched with grief.

One Positive Thing

It was the baby that changed my mind.

Or fetus. If I recall correctly, the rule is that if it can live on its own, it's a baby. That's about six months. But this is Viet Nam; how can you tell? The people are so tiny, newborn babies look like fetuses. Or kittens.

I keep cats at home. Or did; my sister has them now. Three—two calicos and one Heinz-57 tom from the Mason City shelter. Nancy's taking care of them for me. I don't think I'll have an easy time getting them back. Nancy's generous; it's a natural thing with her. She pulls things in, people and animals; if it needs care, it finds her. And it stays. She's had a husband for ten years, and she's only thirty. Three kids of her own and two adopted. And now, my three cats.

I can't compete with Nancy; even my cats will figure that out. I've never felt that urge to give myself completely. Sometimes, when I look at my sister's sweet little dirty-faced kids, I panic. Not that I don't love them—God knows, I love them to death. But they're so present. So real. You can't set out a litter box and leave them for the weekend.

The cats have been my children. Manageable children. I haven't even considered how I'd deal with the real thing. Which makes this all the stranger.

I was flattered when Steve came to me. When he chose me. Because he is who he is, and because I'm no Nancy; people don't seek me out when they need care. But there he was, after another day of blood and frustration, one day too many. It was almost corny; him, standing at the door of my hooch with a bottle of wine. And the next thing I knew, I was no longer the World's Oldest Virgin.

The sex was not painful the first time. It wasn't the stuff of movies, either. I wondered if there was supposed to be more passion, more fire, more desperate grasping and flailing. I didn't have anything to compare it with. It was close. And strong, but quiet; and afterward, I held him, his head pillowed on my breasts. I stroked his fine blond hair and watched him fall asleep, full of those twitchy little tics that pull my heart so when one of Nancy's kids falls asleep in my lap. So this was what it was like, watching a man sleep, I thought. It's like they don't grow up at all.

That was the first time, nearly four months ago. The last time, a week ago—the night before he left—was unsettled, distracted. His body was in my bed, but he was already gone. It was sad and hollow. And I tended my own secret, wrapped myself around it and set us even farther apart. I suppose it was protective instinct—not that I could tell you which of us I was protecting.

It never really was about love—or about sex, for that matter. It was about shelter. Even though he'd been here so much longer than I, this place ground through his skin like sandpaper. I figure that's because doctors are supposed to cure people, surgeons especially. "To Cut is to Cure." He was an artist; he wasn't equipped for the salvage work this place made him do.

Shelter. I am—I was—a loner; maybe he took that for strength. And I was carried away by his attention, his need. I became his shelter—nurturer, *mother*. But it was an act, and I was a fraud. I've seen the pictures of his wife, his two kids. A boy and a girl. No dirt on their faces. He had the family dog, the station wagon, that Christmas-card house with the big, droopy trees dripping with Spanish moss.

I have no illusions. The Steves of this world don't mate with my kind. A surgeon doesn't marry an overweight, over-frank farm girl. He marries the woman in that picture, a tall redhead born to wear a little black dress.

This is why I never told him: he is a good man. He did what he did because he had to; he didn't do it to hurt me. It was a matter of survival. And it's not like I didn't get anything from it; even loners sometimes need comfort.

It's been a week and, to be honest, I miss it. I don't miss Steve. But I miss the comfort.

I knew almost immediately. Granted, I've never gone through this before, but I'm no fool—-two periods late, my breasts even bigger than usual. Sore as they were when I was 12 and they'd just sprouted. And nausea—-God. As bad as Hepatitis—-but I knew it wasn't that, you can't get it twice. I couldn't even stomach my afternoon smoke at first. I remember standing outside the OR airlock, vomiting; Toby Stewart came up, all concerned, "Captain Reedy? Are you okay?" Thank God he's a kid who puts two and two together and gets five.

Steve—you'd expect a doctor to notice. But you'd be amazed, what you can ignore when you don't want to know.

I beat my fists on my stomach, at first. As if that would do something. I lifted heavy loads—-I went out of my way to find hard physical labor. I carried trays of instruments piled on top of each other. For a couple of weeks, nobody in the OR had to put away their own packs–if I wasn't knee-deep in my own cases, I'd grab them and lug them out to the autoclaves.

I knew, even as I denied it, that it would take more than that. I'm a healthy woman, save for my little black lungs. I could jump up and down all day; I could fall down the steps, if there were any around here worth falling down. I could beat myself black and blue. If the caseload and the 24-hour days didn't kill me, nothing I could do would kill what was growing inside me. I could almost see it, cells multiplying two, four, eight, sixteen, a million, two million—-and I knew there was only one way to stop it.

I don't have anything against abortion, philosophically. But philosophy be damned; here, it would've been simply impossible to do. The 22nd Surg is a small town, even smaller than where I grew up. To have booked myself into an OR room on a slack day—-if we *had* a slack day—-would have been like standing in the middle of the compound and announcing that I was pregnant. Even Toby would've figured out who the father was. There are precious few secrets around here.

So I asked the C.O. for two days off in a row. I didn't tell him why, of course, but he took one look at my face and agreed without discussion. I've looked haggard since my first day here, and being pregnant hasn't helped. Funny—Nancy blooms with her babies. Her skin glows, her smile glows, it's as if she carries a diamond inside. I, on the other hand, look like I've died.

I sent a letter to an old friend in the Navy, Marsha, who works on the big hospital ship in Da Nang harbor. I sent it, sealed and taped, with a medevac pilot. She wrote back, a note full of concern, and assured me they could schedule me in. They'd be discreet.

The day after I received her note, two days before I was to go, we had a mass casualty. A grenade went off in a massage parlor, a big place on the outskirts of Hue that catered to GIs; some of our corpsmen go. I wouldn't be surprised if a soldier blew the place up, someone who was unhappy with the service.

The choppers landed, and we cut grenade flak out of young women and sewed them together. There was little time to eat, no time to rest. I'd taken to keeping crackers from the mess hall in my shift pocket, next to my Winstons; I nibbled them on the sly between cases to keep my nausea in check.

I was assisting Steve when I found myself looking down at the baby. Reb Orcutt was debriding dead tissue down at the mother's legs; Crispo, a plastic surgeon back in The World, was suturing a rip in her eyelid. Steve had opened the woman's belly, then her uterus, hunting for a piece of shrapnel.

And there it was, the baby. A little girl, fully-formed, about as big as Steve's fist, still inside her mother.

I stared at this little person with her new-kitten face—curled so efficiently, so tightly, head-down in her mother's womb—as I handed my lover clamps and sponges.

Steve touched the baby with tender gloved fingers, moved her tiny arm, probed softly along her ribs—they were no bigger than

67

a chicken's. When he looked up at me, his eyes were shiny above his blue mask.

Sensitivity, vulnerability—here, these are defects, holes in your hide where the horror of everything can seep through. I saw the muscle twitch in the angle of his jaw, at the edge of his mask. He didn't have to say a thing.

I look down and see the hole in the baby's side. There isn't much blood; the amniotic fluid has thinned it, and it's been sucked away by the suction tip I've propped in the corner of the wound. There is just a jagged puncture in her tiny side. And in it, a little dark point of metal that, when the mother breathes, catches the light from the big lamp over us. The baby, so neatly folded, everything in miniature—clamped eyelids, clenched fists, feet no bigger than my thumbnail—is dead.

"Reb?" I said. Orcutt looked up from the leg and cocked his eyebrow at me. "Can you take over up here for me?" He dropped his mayo scissors on the drapes and moved up, gloved hands folded together.

Steve glanced at me, then moved both hands to the baby. I didn't wait to see him scoop the little girl out; I couldn't. I ran for the side airlock, tearing off my mask.

I made it outside just in time to throw up in the dirt. Nothing but crackers and bile, but it was thorough and cleansing; it felt as if I had forced something terrible out of myself. When I stood up at last, my legs surprised me; they were strong. I stripped off my gloves and my paper OR gown and walked to the helipad, which was empty for a change. I sat down on the tarmac and I screamed, screamed my head off, cursed at the sky, the pavement, men, the war—

And I cried.

It was the first time I had ever cried in Viet Nam, and it seemed to call up all those tears I'd bottled up, six and one-half months of them. A river; a storm.

When it finally let up, I felt light. Warm.

It was a strange feeling, so unexpected. I lit up a cigarette, sucked in the smoke. It tasted like salvation, and I smoked it down to the filter, then got up and brushed myself off.

By now, the dead baby would be gone from her mother, lying in a saline basin or wrapped up in drapes. Just something to be thrown away. I touched my belly and I pictured a cluster of cells, faintly baby-like—the fetus, my baby-to-be, floating uncrowded, enjoying the freedom. No need yet to fold itself into a fist.

Amid all the death, one positive thing. I wiped a hand over my face as I started back to the OR, but the tears were dry.

The Exorcism

The Lieutenant came to the old Buddhist grave behind the mess hall, as she usually did on her days off, to enjoy a quiet afternoon alone. She slathered suntan oil on her arms and legs, then seated herself comfortably on the low, circular stone wall, took a sip of gin-and-tonic, opened Sartre's *The Age of Reason*, and slipped immediately into a silken-sweet oblivion beyond the teeth of the war.

Daniel had just refused to lend Mathieu 5,000 francs for Marcelle's abortion, suggesting instead that Mathieu marry his mistress ("Are you crazy?" asked Mathieu), when the Lieutenant, gnawing intently on her thumbnail, felt a vague unease. She glanced up to find an old man staring at her. He was completely naked.

The Lieutenant leapt up, nearly spilling her drink, clutching the book to her hammering heart.

The old man was not exposing himself: he was squatting in the Vietnamese style, and his long hands dangled between his spread knees, hiding his crotch in their shadow. He watched her mournfully from the other side of the small burial mound, not five feet away.

"What do you want?" the Lieutenant demanded.

The old man said nothing.

The Lieutenant dropped her book on the little wall. She pulled off her glasses, polished them with the tail of her madras shirt, and re-adjusted them on her nose. He was still there. His bald head gleamed in the mid-day sunlight, smooth except for a deep, unnatural indentation above his right temple. His wispy grey chin-whiskers scraggled down to the middle of a chest that revealed every rib. His skin was both brown and impossibly sallow, almost translucent, and his butterflied knees were fleshless knobs. His eyes sparkled sadly, black stars in a net of wrinkles. They drew her in, set her off-balance.

The Lieutenant caught her breath. "If it's money you want, I don't have any on me," she said. "Go away. Please."

The old man remained silent.

"Jesus," muttered the Lieutenant. She assessed him carefully. He was obviously crazy—even in Viet Nam, people wore clothes. But not menacing: he was ancient and sere, his bones so delicate that she could have easily snapped them. No threat at all.

"What do you want?" she repeated. She picked up her cup of gin-and-tonic and held it out, took a step toward him. He neither reached for it nor rejected it, but continued to watch her. Without fear; without curiosity. There was only a deep, wounded regard, and something the Lieutenant could feel but not quite grasp; a bemused unreality that quickened her pulse and made her legs feel rubbery.

She closed her eyes. "Fuck this," she said.

She retreated and snatched up her book, stepped over the wall, strode away.

She turned back when she reached the mess tent.

The old man was not there.

The hair on her bare arms rose. She stared at the vacant grave mound, and took a gulp of her drink.

Over the next two days, the hospital was inundated with casualties—GIs, ARVNs, civilians. The Lieutenant worked long, bloody hours until late on the second night, when the pace slackened and she was at last able to slip out to the mess tent for midnight breakfast.

The sky was clear and full of moon. She wandered out behind the tent, carrying a piece of toast and a glass of reconstituted orange juice. She noted gratefully that her favorite gravesite was deserted— had the old man really existed? Maybe not. She sank down on the short wall.

The old man materialized.

The lieutenant dropped her glass. "*Jesus!*" It smashed against the corner of the wall, splattering orange juice on her sneakers.

He squatted where she had seen him before, across the mound from her. His skin gave back the moonlight, the dent in his head shadowed like a third eye socket.

Her heart pounded. "Don't you *sleep?*"

He moved his head slightly, moved his eyes into the light. The pain in them struck her like a blow. She stood up. "You're hungry, right? Is that it?" She held out her toast. "Here. I haven't touched it. Take it." She stepped toward him, bearing the toast like a crucifix, but the space between them stretched and he grew no nearer, and she felt, again, that muzzy sense of being off-kilter.

The old man bowed his head and disappeared, as if touched by a wizard's wand.

The Lieutenant took a long, shaky breath. Her fist was clenched; she opened her fingers slowly, and a crushed lump of toast fell out. She moved to the spot where the old man had been, bent and examined the ground; he had not left so much as a footprint in the dried grass.

"Lieutenant? Are you okay?"

Toby Stewart stood at the grave wall, wide-eyed. He was an OR tech, a slight, timid young man who had worked beside her all day.

She straightened. "I'm fine, Stewart."

"Weren't you talking to somebody, Ma'am?"

"Well, yes—I was talking to the old guy."

Toby shrugged his skinny shoulders. "I didn't see nobody."

"He was right here just a minute ago. You couldn't miss him."

Toby looked confused.

She bristled. "For Chrissakes, Stewart, he was *naked*—don't tell me you didn't see the guy!"

Toby backed away, shaking his head. "I guess I missed him, Lieutenant. It's dark. Sorry—"

"I'm not crazy, Stewart." The Lieutenant sighed. "I've only been here two months. That's not long enough to be crazy. He was *right here.*"

"I'm sure he was, Ma'am," said the tech, his sincerity unnerving.

For several days, the Lieutenant pointedly avoided the grave behind the mess tent. She felt its loss deeply, personally; she missed the comfort of its circular stone wall, the broadest and smoothest of all the graves' on the compound. She missed its location—far enough from the wards and walkways to give her privacy, but close enough so she could see the helicopters and run to meet them. She missed the peaceful, sunny mornings, and the late afternoons, when the long shadow of the mess tent stretched to give her shade. There were few places to hide at the 22nd Surg, and the grave had been hers.

She found herself harboring a growing resentment toward the old man who had so cavalierly taken away her cherished haven.

On her next day off, she gathered her book and a piece of pizza she'd cooked on her electric skillet, and set out for the grave with a new, righteous determination.

She was not surprised to find the old man squatting naked in the glaring sun.

He watched her as she stepped into the walled circle. She spread a paper napkin before him on the top of the burial mound and set the pizza on it. "Eat it, then get out of here," she told him sternly. "*Di-di mau.*" She sat down in her accustomed spot and opened her book.

She read the same paragraph twice, a dozen times, feeling his burning eyes, their penetrating anguish, the wordless invitation to meet them, to fall into them.

She rose and threw up her hands. "I don't know what you want from me," she lamented. "That's genuine Chef Boy-ar-dee pizza—I got the mix from home, for Chrissakes! Eat it—it's good for you. Put some meat on those bones." He said nothing. She planted her fists on her hips. "Look, this is MY grave. All I want is a place where I can read in peace. Is that too much to ask? I mean, you've got the whole damned country!" She gave him a hard look.

The old man squatted, his eyes fastened upon hers. They were filled with sorrow, every sorrow known to humankind funneled into two black wells.

The Lieutenant backed away, squeezed her eyes shut. "If you're trying to spook me, you're wasting your time," she rasped. "I don't believe in ghosts."

But the Lieutenant was, in truth, spooked. The next day, clumsy and glassy-eyed, she fumbled through a chest wound and an amputation, contaminating her gloves three times. She dropped a clamp and two packs of sponges and forgot how to square-knot a suture. The surgeon asked her what was wrong.

"I'm just tired," she said, handing him a clamp he hadn't asked for. "Just really, really tired."

At lunchtime, she ducked into the Medical Holding ward to find Suong, the hospital's main interpreter, who was explaining to an ARVN soldier that he was not permitted to sleep with his wife in his hospital bed. The Lieutenant paced the ward until the young woman had finished, then took her by the elbow and led her outside.

"Do you believe in ghosts?" the Lieutenant asked her.

Suong's eyes grew round. "Ghosts? Spirits? Oh, no. I am Catholic."

The Lieutenant armed sweat from her forehead. She felt unaccountably melancholic and her head hurt. "If you weren't Catholic, would you believe in ghosts?"

Suong looked away. "The old ones say there are spirits."

The Lieutenant sagged against the hot rubber corner of the ward. "If you saw one of these spirits, how would you make it go away?"

"You see a spirit?"

"Oh, no—not me." The Lieutenant forced a laugh. "Of course not. But if someone did, say—if they saw a spirit on, say, a grave? How would they make it go away?"

74

"It is an angry spirit?"

"No. Not angry, I don't think. Sad. Depressed, maybe."

"It is hurting someone?"

The Lieutenant touched her aching forehead. "It's making someone have very bad dreams. So—yes, I guess it's hurting someone. Because the next day, they can't work worth a damn."

Suong pursed her lips. Then she said, "The old ones keep the grave clean. Perhaps the spirit have not a clean grave, make him sad."

The Lieutenant nodded.

"Or—perhaps the spirit is hungry? It have nobody here to give it food?"

"I left it—" The Lieutenant checked herself. "This friend of mine, the one with the bad dreams, she left it food, but it didn't eat."

"This is American food?"

The Lieutenant nodded.

"Perhaps the spirit not like American food."

The Lieutenant considered this.

Suong brightened. "Tomorrow, I bring you Vietnamese food—-number One. Joss stick is good, too."

Suong appeared at the Lieutenant's hooch the next morning at 6 a.m. with a crinkled paper bag. She followed the Lieutenant to the grave, and spread the contents on the wall under the somber gaze of the naked old man.

The interpreter set a tiny, perfect orange and a paper plate of fried egg rolls and little balls of sticky rice on the burial mound. To the Lieutenant's amazement and dismay, the young woman trod on the old man's long, bony toes and, when she jammed two smoldering joss sticks into the ground, nudged her narrow butt into his chest. But the old man neither moved nor reacted; he ignored Suong entirely and continued to give the Lieutenant the full bore of his gaze.

At last, the interpreter stood back and viewed her handiwork. "I do not know if this is good," she said. "I am Catholic."

"It looks great." The Lieutenant watched the old man warily, her stomach in knots. "My friend will like it," she told Suong. "If I believed in spirits, I'd certainly expect it to do the trick."

The next evening after work, the Lieutenant caught up with Suong in the Vietnamese ward. She waited, shifting from foot to foot, while the interpreter explained to a patient that her four grandchildren would have to make do with one electric skillet, because plugging two at once into her bedside outlet had shorted out the ward's lighting. When she finished, the Lieutenant motioned her outside.

"It's all still there," said the Lieutenant.

Suong raised her hands, palms up. "You must know, the spirit do not eat the food like people do. He eat like spirit. He get fat, but food not go away."

"But *he* didn't go away." The Lieutenant grasped Suong's sleeve with trembling fingers. "The old man's still there."

"Oh. That is not good." The interpreter thought for a moment. "Perhaps he need money."

"Money?"

"Spirit money. Not real money—paper, like for Tet. Spirit use money in the other world."

"Where would I get spirit money?"

"I get you some," said Suong. "Perhaps you—your friend—write spirit a letter?"

"A letter? What about?"

"I don't know. I am Catholic, you see."

The Lieutenant nodded. "Of course."

"You tell him perhaps that you respect him and wish him no harm, and that you will keep his grave clean and bring flowers, and he can rest. You put this and money on the grave—perhaps this make him happy, he go away."

"But I can't write Vietnamese."

The interpreter patted her hand. "The spirit do not read like people read. He know what you say."

And so, while the old man watched, the Lieutenant removed the spent joss sticks and ant-caked food. She arranged the red paper bills Suong had given her on the mound, then laid her letter over them and set a flower on top. "There now—you can rest," she told the old man. "Wouldn't you like to rest? Don't you get tired of coming here? Wouldn't you be happier in some nice temple or farmhouse with a bed, friends, people to take care of you?"

The old man said nothing.

"You don't belong here," she said emphatically.

A single tear crept from the lower lid of his right eye. It caught the sun and dropped, tracing silver down his concave cheek.

The Lieutenant crammed her knuckles into her mouth and turned away.

The next day, she was clamping bleeders and snipping dead tissue from what was left of a GI's leg when Toby Stewart stepped into the operating room to tell her that Scully wanted to see her. The Lieutenant looked up blearily, dropping her clamp; a thin stream of blood shot upward, instantly soaking her mask. She wiped at it, contaminating her glove. "Scully? What's he want?"

Toby shrugged. "He just said to stop by the hooch tonight."

She rolled her eyes. "The perfect ending to a perfect day."

Spec 4 Scully had the long, pointed nose and beady eyes of a rodent. The Lieutenant found him singularly unattractive and his sense of humor puerile. But he was a clerk in Administration. One did not ignore the summons of a clerk; clerks processed the paperwork for one's R&R, promotions and potential reassignments.

And so late that night, the Lieutenant crossed the dark, quiet compound and tapped on the door of the EM hooch.

A black tech from Holding led her through a smoky bay full of beds, past a poker game, past a big Spec 4 laboriously penning a letter, to the far corner of the room, where Scully lounged on his cot. He was stripped to the waist, and his hairless concave chest hitched as he sucked on a joint. The bedspread beneath him was an oversized Confederate flag; the shade of his bedside lamp tilted upward to spotlight a display of fist-sized black blobs, each pegged to the wall by a pencil.

"Well, well, well. Comes the pilgrim." Scully removed the joint from his lips and raised his eyebrows at the Lieutenant. "Set yourself down, Ma'am."

She glanced about, but there were no chairs nearby. Scully patted the bed next to him.

"Thanks, but I think I'll stand." She leaned forward and squinted at the wall. "What *is* that?"

"Them's toads, Lieutenant." Scully held the joint up to her.

She waved it away. "Toads? You mean, poison toads?"

"The same." He grinned toothily.

"You've speared them with pencils."

He pulled a mosquito clamp from his pocket and snapped the end of the joint in its tip. "It's an art, Lieutenant. You gotta catch 'em without touching 'em."

"Charming," she said. "You wanted to see me?"

He took a last puff on the clamped roach, held the smoke in, then said, "I hear you got a ghost problem."

"Who told you that?"

His grin split wide. "I never divulge my sources, Lieutenant."

She tipped up her glasses and rubbed her eyes. "For your information, I don't have a 'ghost' problem. I have an old man problem. But yeah, I'd like him to go away."

Scully sat up languidly. He raised his eyes, to her waist, to her compact, blood-streaked bosom—where they lingered a second too long for her taste—to her face. "Lieutenant, I am prepared to make that happen."

"Oh? And how much will this cost me?"

"Aw, Lieutenant. What makes you think I wouldn't do it for

free, out of the kindness of my heart?"

She yawned. "Cut the shit, Scully."

"Word is, you just got a shipment of pizza mixes."

The Lieutenant sighed. "That's the word."

"Four boxes, and I make the old man go bye-bye."

"Bullshit. I only have six left, to last me for the rest of the month. I could spare three, max." She surveyed him with distaste. "Frankly, why should I believe *you* can do what I haven't been able to do? You might be a clerk, but you're not a magician."

He lifted a finger. "I've got the ways and means, Lieutenant. I've got the *ways* and *means*."

"Three. On delivery––meaning you actually manage to convince the old man to go home. Wherever that is."

Scully pulled a petrified toad from his wall and spun it idly on its pencil skewer. "You surely do drive a hard bargain, Lieutenant." He smiled toothily, terribly. "I'll meet you behind the mess tent tomorrow night at midnight?"

She frowned. "You're not going to hurt him, are you?"

"Now, now, Lieutenant. You can't hurt a ghost."

"He's not a ghost. He's just some disoriented old codger. You hurt him, absolutely no pizza mix."

Scully raised his eyebrows. "He's a disoriented old codger that Toby can't see."

The Lieutenant flicked a glance across the room at the poker game, where Stewart was playing with four other men. She said in a low voice, "As much as I dearly love Toby, if you put his pants on backward, he'd never find his dick. I wouldn't call him a reliable source of information."

Again, the toothy smile. "What about Suong?"

The Lieutenant folded her arms. "Midnight, Scully. Be there."

The Lieutenant arrived at the grave promptly at midnight. The moon was on the wane, but she could still see the old man squatting on the far side of the mound. The letter she had written sat unopened in the center of the grave; she snatched it up and collected the red spirit money, feeling rather than seeing the accusation in his shaded eyes. She sat down on the wall and regarded him—the reflective baldness of his pate, with its indentation; his sparse, shadowy beard; his knobbed knees. "Well, this is it," she told him. "You're out of here." His black eyes gleamed from their dark sockets.

She looked away quickly, down at her hands, twiddled her fingers, wished she smoked. Where the hell was Scully?

She glanced up at the old man. "I really don't understand. I mean, why me?" She steeled herself and met the glimmer of black pupils. "I didn't do anything," she said. "Hell—I even voted for McCarthy."

The eyes mocked her sadly.

Her throat tightened. "Look—I needed the money." She shrugged. "My loan ran out. They paid a whole year of school—and the recruiter, he said I wouldn't have to come here—"

His left eye twinkled.

"It's not *funny*, damn it!" She shifted on the stone, which had become lumpy, oddly unfamiliar. Uncomfortable. Her eyes stung, but she stared defiantly into the tragic mask of the old man's face. "I didn't make this happen. This is not my fault. Nothing here is my fault. Nothing, you understand? *Nothing!*"

"I surely do believe you, Lieutenant," said a voice behind her.

She turned; Scully clicked on a large flashlight and held it beneath his chin; the beam bounced ghoulishly off the bottom of his nose, his cheekbones and eyebrows.

He wore a fraying chenille bathrobe and a Vietnamese conical hat. "Ceremonial garb. What do you think?" He held out the robe's skirt. "You can't see it too good here, but it's yellow in the light. Closest I've got to a saffron robe. Like it?"

"Charming."

"I borrowed it from Mina Griswold." He held up his hand.

"Don't you worry, Lieutenant—I told her it was for a skit we were doing for a farewell party."

"I appreciate your discretion, Scully."

"I appreciate your appreciation, Ma'am." He pulled a long envelope from the robe's bosom and focused the flashlight beam on it. The Lieutenant saw dollops of sealing wax and penned curlicues. "Did this myself." He puffed his scrawny chest. "Gooks love stuff that looks official. Now—where's the altar?"

She pointed. The old man watched balefully.

Scully hiked up his robe and climbed over the little wall. He waved his envelope through the air with a great dramatic flourish, placed it precisely atop the grave mound, bowed three times, and sang in a grating nasal voice: "Oh, I wish I wa-as in the land of cotton—"

"That'll do, Scully," said the Lieutenant. She glanced at the old man—

And her heart stood still.

He was holding the envelope in both hands, as if it were a precious gift. His dark eyes moved from it to her face; there was irony in them, and something else—pity? He bowed his dented bald head—

And vanished.

Her jaw dropped. "Jesus, Scully. Did you see that?"

"Didn't see a thing, Lieutenant."

"Yeah, right." She pointed to the mound. "The old guy took your letter."

"Oh?" Scully played the flashlight beam over the dry grass and brought it to rest—on the envelope. "What the hell, Lieutenant. You say it's gone, it's gone. An officer never lies. I'll take my pizza mixes, if you don't mind."

"It *was* gone, Scully. I swear to God."

"Aw, Lieutenant. You know you don't believe in God." He took off his hat and scratched his buzz-cut head. "Three boxes, thank you kindly."

She handed him a paper bag. "What was in that letter, Scully?"

"That's 'need to know' only, Lieutenant."

"Cut the shit. What was in it?"

He shined his light into the bag and peeked in. "What I did was, I asked myself, Self: if you was a gook, what's the one thing would make you really, truly happy? And I had the ways and means—so that's what I gave him."

"Which was?"

He darted his flashlight beam, once again, to the envelope on the mound. "Ask your ghost. If he lets you read it, though, you got to promise me you'll keep your mouth shut for a week, 'til they make the official announcement."

She stepped to the center of the tomb and picked up the envelope, snapped the seals with her fingernail. The paper inside bore the letterhead of the I-Corps medical command.

Scully handed her the flashlight, and the Lieutenant trained its beam on the letter. She looked at the clerk in disbelief. "This is an order to close down the hospital," she said. "Effective next month." She shook her head. "You've got to be kidding."

"Could be. Army's known for its sense of humor."

She examined the paper again, read and re-read it. "Does this mean—they'll send us home?"

Scully gave a quick, ugly bark of a laugh. "My, my, Lieutenant—how you do take on. But don't you fret—I just know they're gonna send you someplace nice." He winked. "Maybe someplace with a beach." He lifted the letter from her fingers, refolded it, and tucked it into the bosom of his robe. "But you didn't hear none of this from me."

When Scully left, the Lieutenant walked slowly to the spot where the old man had squatted. She knew there was no way she could be certain—but she was: she would never see the old man again. The grave was hers. No more nightmares and daydreams. She bent down and ran her hand over the dried grass, waiting for the relief, the happiness.

But there was only an inexplicable sense of loss.

Don't Mean Nothing

The little black private smoothed out the mail notice and grimaced. "It's back there—we put it in a cooler." He jerked his thumb over his shoulder, at the shelf that ran the length of the mail room's back wall. A large styrofoam cooler sat in the corner, at a self-conscious distance from the heaps of packages and manila envelopes. "Tell you, Organ, I for one am damned glad you finally got here. I was afraid we'd have to pack this up with the rest of the unclaimed shit and stick it on the chopper tomorrow. Oh—don't forget your mail."

Reb Orcutt took two envelopes from the private—a tape from his mother and his bank statement—stuffed them in the pocket of his fatigue pants, and walked behind the counter. He lifted the lid on the styrofoam cooler, then immediately dropped it. Even in that split-second, the reek was staggering. "What the fuck?"

"Don't know what it is, man, but it's all yours. Don't open it in here, huh?"

Orcutt carted the cooler out of the mailroom at arm's length. He carried it to the helipad and set it down on the tarmac. He gulped a great double-lungful of hot, dusty air, held it in, and removed the lid.

The box had been about a foot square and eight inches high before it had bulged up at the top and crumpled on one side. He lifted it carefully from the cooler; the sodden cardboard on the bottom felt dead and slick, as if it had been dipped in jello. He let go of his breath, sucked in again. But even though he kept his nostrils resolutely closed, he could taste it in the air. A pungent carrion heat, peppered with mold.

He tore off the top of the package, which bore his father's return address, the Baton Rouge apartment where the old man had lived since the divorce three years ago.

The box was full of blood and entrails.

Reb gagged. Eyes watering, he glanced down to see a white metal disk poking from the red and pink gore. He gingerly picked it out. A pair of noisy flies circled, landed on its crusted top; he brushed them away and wiped at the disk with a sticky fingertip.

It was a lid. Stamped on top were the words: LOUISIANA QUEEN SHRIMP COCKTAIL.

Fuck, thought Reb Orcutt.

He dumped the package back into the cooler; what used to be a dozen jars of his favorite midnight snack plopped into the styrofoam, glass grinding, metal caps clacking, gelatinous, half-rotted seafood dropping from the cardboard, flies—now a battalion of them—diving after. He shook the jar-lid off his fingers and into the mess, crammed the top onto the cooler, and rose to his feet.

The dumb fuck—sending glass jars of shrimp cocktail through the mail. Jesus!—drunken sonovabitch had to've bought 'em outa the refrigerator *section of the supermarket. Anybody else'd consider that a* hint.

How typical, he reflected, grinding his teeth, that the guy who hadn't done shit for him his whole life should finally try to do a good deed—and fuck it up beyond recognition. He tossed the cooler into the trash barrel next to the room-sized metal conex container where they used to keep bodies for evac—now, it held part of the Medical Cases ward—and stomped back to his hooch.

Fuck, he needed a drink.

* * *

He knew the minute he heard his mother's voice on the scratchy tape that something was wrong. There was a forced smile in her tone; he could almost picture it on her face. She began with the usual pleasantries—his sister was just fine; the dogs missed him; Uncle Cal had bagged them a couple of rabbits for dinner. Then, there was *the*

84

pause. Reb braced himself.

"Jeremiah," her strained smiling voice said, "I wish there was a better way to tell you this."

Again, *the pause*.

"Your father went home to God two days ago."

Reb punched the *Stop* button. He rewound the tape—too far, then brought it back.

"Your father went home to God two days ago."

He punched *Stop* again and sat still for a moment, digesting this information.

Home to God.

He pictured the old man, as he inevitably did, ugly drunk, slapping the shit out of him for no good reason but the feel of it. Home to God. He thought about the shrimp cocktail, rotting and bubbling in its corrugated cardboard carton in the mailroom while his father, presumably, did the same, and a hard, cold hatred knotted his gut. He pressed *Play*.

"Your Uncle George found him in his apartment—he hadn't showed up to the diner two days running, and your Uncle George, he thought there must be something, uh, wrong. So he took his key and opened the door, and there he was—" Her voice wavered slightly—or was it the tape? "Just laying there on the floor next to the telephone, just like he was gonna call somebody. Looks like he must've had a shock." Pause. "Now, I know he wudden't much of a daddy to you, Jeremiah." A heavy sigh. "But like the Bible says, nobody but the Good Lord can judge a man—"

Choppers. He snapped the machine off and cocked his ear. Yes, choppers. Coming this way; converging on the pad. The big ones, come to take away the three wards they'd packed up yesterday.

He looked down at the machine, pressed *Eject*, and took out the cassette. He dropped it next to his bunk, stood up, and stomped on it—once, twice, three times, the heel of his jungle boot cracking, then splintering the casing, brown magnetic tape spooling out in a loose

85

spiral. And again, and again he came down on it, in rhythm to the beat of the chopper blades, now landing on the pad next to what used to be the triage unit. Landing in the middle of what now looked like some giant kid's floor after he'd kicked apart his play village. Humungous tinker toys, roof sections from a Log Cabin set. Pipes and plywood sheets and deflated rubber Quonset "bubbles," folded under hooped steel ribs. And, everywhere, those huge metal boxes.

As if all this packing shit—all this *leaving* shit—wasn't depressing enough.

Fucker, thought Reb Orcutt. *That a fucker like you can die a peaceful death is proof positive that there is no God.*

He kicked the remains of the cassette under his bunk and headed out to the helipad.

* * *

The sun pulled sweat from their bare backs, as the five men heaved yet another rubber wall segment into its metal conex. Toby Stewart, Reb Orcutt's best buddy and the only other remaining OR tech, stood back and rubbed at his streaming forehead with the back of a peeling forearm. "Think about it, Organ—somebody took all this stuff out and put it together, what—three, four years ago? And now, here we are, putting it back in the boxes it came in—" They ducked and turned away as yet another jumbo helicopter dropped down on the pad, its rotors beating a storm of dust and small rocks over them. Toby pulled a crushed cigarette pack from his fatigue pants and picked out a smoke. "Sheeee-it, man. Don't mean nothing." He pushed the pack toward Reb Orcutt.

"Thanks, man." Orcutt fished a squashed cigarette from the pack with two fingers and stuck it in his mouth, then took the book of matches Toby handed him.

The others—Harper, Nealon and Scully—trotted over. The chopper's rotors machined to a stop.

"Hey, Organ-man." Nealon scratched at his square, fuzzy brown belly. "Hear you're headed up to the DMZ."

Orcutt nodded. "You?"

"Long Binh. Me and Harper, man."

Harper grinned, all white teeth in a gaunt and very black face.

"Can't tear the twins apart," said Nealon. "Auggie Wray's off to Long Binh, too. Left this morning."

"Good man," said Harper.

Scully nodded, gave a thumbs-up sign.

"Good man," agreed Nealon. "How 'bout you, Tobe?" he said. "They gonna let you DEROS?"

Scully spat. "Hell no—I saw his papers." Scully was a clerk in Headquarters, he saw everybody's papers. "They're sending him to the Big City. He's gonna have to wear a real uniform."

Toby shrugged skinny, splotchy shoulders. Eleven months in the tropics, and he still couldn't tan. "You know the army, man. They're gonna get every blessit second out of me. But hey—don't mean nothin', man."

Nealon lit up a cigarette of his own and handed one to Harper, one to Scully. "You know it, man. That's the truth. But Saigon ain't far from Long Binh—-stop in, we'll have us a reunion."

"They're sending me out tomorrow, man," said Toby. "So you guys'll have to finish up without me."

"Ah, man," said Nealon in mock dismay. "You just gonna cut out, let us slaves do the hard stuff."

"Hah!" Scully blew out smoke; with his squinty eyes and sharp nose, he reminded Orcutt of a weasel. "I'm still here—-even the white guys gotta work. Even," he said, puffing his narrow chest, "the *clerks* gotta work."

"Work?" said Harper. "Thisshere ain't no work, man. It's *Phu Bai.* An' Phu Bai—"

"Is All Right," Nealon, Toby and Scully chimed in smoky unison.

Scully flicked his ash. "Hey, Organ—heard you got you a care package from Daddy." Scully gave Orcutt the creeps; he was from Alabama, and he thought that being from the south made him Reb Orcutt's special com-fucking-padre. It frosted Orcutt that he had to be civil to the little bastard. You didn't piss off a clerk in this man's Army; you never knew what might become of your paperwork. Orcutt had heard Scully was being posted down in Chu Lai—which was fine, because it was a good, healthy distance from Orcutt's next duty station. He sucked at his cigarette and said nothing.

"No shit," said Toby. "Your old man?"

Orcutt gave him a look that said he didn't want to discuss it, particularly not with the weasel around.

But subtleties were lost on Toby. "I thought you and your old man didn't connect."

Scully grinned, picked a piece of tobacco off a tooth. "Oh, he done conNECted, all right—Harrison says what the man sent stunk so bad, he couldn't light a match, figured it'd blow the mail shack sky high. What'd he send you, a dead cat?"

Toby looked sincerely interested. "Really? He sent you a *dead cat*??"

Orcutt ground his teeth.

"You said the old man was weird, but that's just plain *sick*," said Toby.

The mess sergeant, a big man, shirtless and sweating rivers into his ample waistband, approached the group. He was the Man In Charge at the moment, and even at ten feet, his face told them there was business to be tended to.

"Shit." Nealon rolled his eyes. "Simon Legree." He nodded to Harper and Scully, and they moved away.

Reb Orcutt tossed aside his cigarette and stepped toward yet another puddle of flattened rubber.

At his elbow, Toby said, "Did your daddy really send you a dead cat?"

"Shrimp cocktail."

Toby whistled. "Shrimp cocktail?"

"Whole box of it."

"Cans? they put it in cans?"

Orcutt threw him a look. "Glass jars."

"Shee-it, man. Don't you have to keep that stuff in a refrigerator or freezer or something?"

Orcutt seized a corner of the rubber—a segment that had once belonged to the Prisoners' ward—and yanked it out straight. "Good idea to."

"Man. The man must've been incredibly, truly shitfaced, huh?"

Reb Orcutt looked Toby in the eye. "Fucker's incredibly, truly dead, man."

"Huh?"

Orcutt sighed and squatted in the dust. "The old man's gone to hell. Dead."

"He sent you shrimp cocktail after he was *dead*?"

Orcutt snorted. "Yeah. Ghost shrimp cocktail. Shrimp cocktail from *beyond*." He stood up and stretched his back.

"I'm sorry, man. That was incredibly, truly stupid, wasn't it?"

Orcutt yanked at the rubber and backed up.

Toby picked up his own corner and walked backward. "You know, man—I'm sorry. About your old man, I mean."

Reb Orcutt stared down at the flat olive-green rubber. He saw the house, the falling-down porch. His mother, with her loose jowls and tight smile, standing on that porch, work-knotted hands wrapped around the splintered post. A flat, dry, ugly spot in a swamp, mosquitoes big as buzz-saws—inertia as home, home as stagnation. "I'm not," he said.

"Huh?"

"Sorry. I'm not. He should've died nineteen years ago. Done us all a big favor."

Toby laid his corner down, shifted on his feet.

89

"What the fuck," said Reb Orcutt. He sat down on the deflated rubber "bubble" and stared up at Toby, his hand over his eyes to shield them from the sun. "Don't mean nothin', right?"

* * *

The night was moonless; here and there, lone electrical bulbs dangled from poles and threw a harsh, shifting, incomplete light over the packing rubble. Toby Stewart and Reb Orcutt sat on the high shipping platform behind the Operating Room, swinging their legs, smoking and gulping Budweiser from long-necked bottles. The Operating Room was one of only two rubber "bubbles" left standing. A dim light still shone through the window of its door behind them, even though the place was scheduled for deflation tomorrow.

"S'pose they'll stick it in the chopper with me?" said Toby.

"Maybe. Make sense, wouldn't it?"

"Where's all this shit going to, man?"

Orcutt shrugged.

"I mean, they said they wasn't going to use it anymore." Toby dug a stubby nail into the label of his Budweiser.

"I dunno. Maybe send it to Bangladesh."

Toby took a swig. "Think so?"

Orcutt said nothing. He sucked on his cigarette and tried to remember the last time he'd seen his father. Had he seen the Baton Rouge apartment? He tried to recall where it was, what it looked like, but nothing came to mind. Maybe he hadn't. Maybe he hadn't seen him since the divorce.

No, there was the time the old man came back to the house. It was before Reb Orcutt had shipped out. Maybe before Basic, even. It was when the old man'd busted the front window with a rock, and Reb Orcutt had called the cops. But that'd happened before, too, even before the divorce, when his mother had kicked the old man out on his ass that time.

Toby's voice cut into his thoughts. "–Trouble is, I don't *know* anybody in Saigon. And I'm too Short to *get* to know anybody–"

Orcutt chugged the last of his beer, reached into the cooler and grabbed another. He snubbed his cigarette butt out beside him on the wooden dock, and tossed it into the void below. Somewhere above and behind him, a bug whirred like a miniature helicopter, then pinged away into hot silence.

He glanced at Toby's troubled profile. "So do your month and leave," he said. He closed his eyes. Oh. Wow. No, it was last year, he saw the old man. On his birthday. How on God's earth could he forget that? The old man had brought him–

Toby upended his bottle, threw it out into the darkness. It exploded against something metal with a particularly satisfying shivery crash. "I dunno, man." He swung his legs hard, back and forth, back and forth. Very softly, he said, "I dunno if I can."

"Just do what I do, man. Don't think about being *here*, think about what you'll do *after*."

Toby pulled another bottle out of the cooler, bit off the cap–

Orcutt cringed. He hated it when Toby opened beer bottles with his teeth. Made his spine hurt–made a little electrical charge travel right down it.

Toby set his bottle down and pulled out a crumpled cigarette pack. "Another butt?"

Orcutt fished a cigarette from the pack, straightened it out, and bent down to the match Toby was holding. "Thanks, man." He inhaled the smoke, held it in, pushed it out through his nose. On his nineteenth birthday last year, exactly five days before he boarded his flight to Viet Nam, the old man had brought him a little store-bought birthday cake. No name on the damned thing; just "Happy Birthday." No candles, either. Reb Orcutt had thought, at the time, that it must've been one of the day-old things from the big supermarket in Baton Rouge. A dead-looking whitish frosting, one blue rose–blue, for chrissakes–that seemed to be melting around the edges.

He had lifted the lid on the limp cardboard box and taken just a small look. Just a small look. But it was enough to burn the colors, the tired look of that miserable cake, in his memory. And then the old man had smiled his snag-toothed, sheepish, friends-now-ain't-we smile.

"Thing is," said Toby, "I dunno what I'm gonna do when I get back, man. All I know to do is *this*. And I don't want to do *this*. I'm–" He took a swig, sucked at his cigarette, blew a puff of smoke. "Sheee-it, man. I'm–I dunno. Tired."

"So marry that girl of yours. Have some kids." Orcutt's eyes rested on the bottle in Toby's hands, but saw the old man's unbalanced, pathetic grin. That's what had done it. Wasn't the cake–although that would've been reason enough. No. It was the smile.

"Organ, I don't even *know* her anymore. I mean, she don't know me; we might not even fit." He hung his head. "Lately, man, I been having these thoughts."

Something in Toby's voice brought Reb Orcutt to full attention. He put his hand on Toby's shoulder. It was trembling, as if the air were chilled, rather than oven-hot. "What thoughts, Tobe?"

Toby shrugged. "Thoughts––and dreams." He took a long, deep breath; there was a hitch in the middle of it.

Shit, man–don't go all soft on me. Reb Orcutt clenched his teeth and forced himself to keep his hand on Toby's shoulder.

Toby cleared his throat. "Remember that guy, hit a mine, we cut off both his legs and his arm–"

"Which guy's that?"

Toby didn't catch the humor. "Maybe a month ago. That guy."

Orcutt squeezed Toby's shoulder. As if he could forget the guy; got half his prick blown off, too. He'd thought, *if it was me like that, kill me now, man.*

"I see him sometimes–"

Jesus.

"At night. I dream––lately. A lot. He waves that bloody arm at me, no hand–" Toby took another swig of Budweiser and stifled a sob.

"Man, you must think I'm a real straaaa-aaange fucker, Organ."

"You *are* a strange fucker, Tobe."

In spite of himself, Toby gave a snaggled breath, a not-quite giggle.

Orcutt pushed his advantage. "Man, I don't have a doubt in the world what I'm gonna do when I get out of this-fucking-man's army," he said. "I'm going straight to El Lay."

"L.A.?" Toby sniffed and sat up straight. "Why L.A.?"

"I'm gonna get me in the movies, my good man." Reb Orcutt smiled toothily, a movie smile. He drew on the cigarette, blew a smoke ring, barely visible in the meager window light. "With a face like this, who could resist me?"

"Yeah, right." A giggle—real, this time, if slight.

Orcutt relaxed. He watched the kid flick his cigarette off the dock; the night was so quiet that Orcutt could hear it tick against the pavement eight feet below. "Yep," he said. "I'm going to El Lay, man. Find me one of them James Bond women." He emptied his bottle and held it over the edge of the dock. "Geronimo," he said, and let it go. Amazingly, it did not shatter. He whistled and peeked over the edge, but all he could see was darkness.

"It's the way you dropped it," said Toby. "I've had that happen before—you know, you drop a glass off the table once, it breaks? You drop another one, it bounces?" He shook his head. "Must be some physics law, but I never did take physics, so I don't know."

Orcutt reached around to the cooler and extracted another bottle. "So." He pulled his churchkey from his pocket and popped the lid. "You want, you can come with me. There's plenty of James Bond women for both of us in El Lay."

"Yeah. Right." Toby snorted.

Orcutt took a deep drink. He was beginning to feel good, really good. Fan-fucking-tastic. He congratulated himself on pushing Toby past his funk. Best to keep charging, though. He said, "You know what? I just figured out the last time I saw my old man. Know what he was doing?"

Toby shook his head.

Reb Orcutt snuffed out his cigarette and pressed his beer bottle to his forehead. It wasn't cold; the ice in the cooler had melted. "My old man," he said slowly, "was bouncing on his ass down the front steps of my Mamma's porch."

Toby said nothing; he waited for Orcutt to explain.

"He was bouncing down the steps on his sad, skinny ass, following my birthday cake. Both of 'em had help, don't ya know, getting down those steps."

Toby emptied his bottle, threw it out in a long, high arc, and listened to it shatter.

"I wish you'd of seen it—the cake was in this bakery-type box, you know? Lid with big flaps and all?"

Toby nodded.

"And I left it right in the box." He struggled to his feet. "And—" He pantomimed a football drop—"I drop-kicked the sucker—*poom.*" His foot snapped up. "My old man durned near loaded his britches. Didn't go too far, though." He frowned, balanced on one foot, snapped a kick again. "Weight was wrong. Shifted in the box or something. Just went *ploop*, flopped over, hit the step, plopped down. Old man turned around to see, and I—" Once again, he snapped his kick. "Right in the ass. Felt *good*, man. Felt de-fuckin-licious."

"You better step back, man."

Reb Orcutt balanced again on one foot, inches from the edge, put both arms out. "What'sa matter, son—make you nervous?"

Toby reached toward him, but Orcutt smacked his hand away.

"Hey—that *you* up there, Mighty Organ?" Scully's high, thin voice drifted up to them from below.

Orcutt squinted and could barely make out the rim of his close-cropped blond head in the semi-darkness. Shit. He lowered his foot. "Go fuck yourself," he mumbled.

"What's that?" came the voice.

94

"Come up through the OR," said Toby. "It's open."

"*No.*" Reb Orcutt's voice was loud and decisive. "We're having a party of two, thank you, and you ain't one."

"Organ, that's not nice," said Toby, with that annoying sincerity of his. "I'm out of here tomorrow, and I'd kind of like to have a drink with him."

Orcutt positioned himself immediately at the edge of the dock and lifted his leg and both arms once again. "Suit yourself," he said.

"Organ." Toby's voice was pleading. "Don't do that. It makes me—"

The OR door behind them popped open; Reb Orcutt twisted his head toward it, toward the dim light in the window next to it. *Fucking weasel—*

Shit!

What the *fuck*?!

It was a smooth, short fall, and when he struck the pavement, he was amazed that there was no pain, just a jarring *whump*, air whacked out of his lungs. And a snap, a sound with no feel. He opened his eyes; panic flared, then ebbed; he wasn't blind. It was just the darkness beneath the loading dock.

"*Organ.*"

Above him. Toby.

"What the *fuck*??" This was Scully. Up there.

Orcutt's anger flared. "Fucker," he said to himself.

"What the *fuck*!" said Scully. "What the *fuck* was he *doing*?"

"Organ, say something!" Toby's voice wailed.

Orcutt reached a hand down to his side, below his waist. His hand felt his hip, but his hip didn't feel his hand. He groped; a bag, a bag full of something that took up space, something dead and heavy that wasn't him.

He began to sweat.

He willed his leg to move; it wasn't there.

"Don't move, Organ."

He worked his fingers under himself; dampness. Beer? Sweat? *Man*, he thought. He swallowed hard. *I'm drunker than I thought.* In a couple of minutes, he'd be sitting on his bunk, laughing his ass off about this. Orcutt closed his eyes. He heard footsteps—running, a stumble, a curse. A panting gasp. A hand, hot and damp on his bare shoulder. He turned his head, scraped his nose on the pavement; Toby bent over him, a silhouette against the faint light tracing the compound beyond.

"Organ—are you all right? Organ—*say* something—"

He felt Toby's hand walk down his back, down to his waistband, then evaporate.

"Can you feel this, Organ?"

"Feel what."

Toby stood up, looked up. "*Get* someone!" His voice was ragged. "*Get someone!*"

"Oh, man." Scully, still above them. "It's only what, seven, eight feet?"

"Scully! *Get someone, Goddammit!*"

Orcutt knifed his hand down, farther, into the dampness below him, a flesh shovel beneath a packed duffel; his knuckles rasped against the pavement. Damp cloth, form and weight; no life. Foreign. Not him.

"Oh, Jesus, Organ," said Toby. "Oh, Holy Christ—"

Orcutt stretched his arm to the side. His fingers brushed something hard, smooth, cylindrical; it rolled, but he caught it, grabbed it. An empty beer bottle. He began to shake with silent mirth. His upper parts; nothing below, which struck him, suddenly, as hilarious.

"Oh, Jesus God, Organ—don't cry—"

Orcutt opened his mouth, and laughter poured out. "Don't—don't—don't—"

"What? What?" Toby's voice was frantic. "*What??*"

"Don't mean no—noth—"

PART II

Chu Lai

Perquisites

"Get real, Scully." The Lieutenant squinted at the scrawny clerk. He stood at rigid attention on the white sand path in front of the Operating Room Quonset, his right hand leveled at his forehead.

"Rule book says I'm to initiate the salute, Lieutenant. And you're to give it back." Scully grinned, his small eyes gleaming as if he had guessed the punch line to a private joke.

"Fuck you, Private Scully." The Lieutenant raised her middle finger solemnly to the temple of her eyeglasses. "It's bad enough I've got to salute my superiors here, never mind my inferiors."

Scully snorted appreciatively. He and the Lieutenant went 'way back—a full four months, to the days when they had both been stationed at the now-closed 22nd Surg in Phu Bai. "In two days," he said, "You're gonna have even more inferiors."

"Which means what?"

"You're gonna get your little piece of silver." He pulled a paper from his shirt pocket, unfolded it and held it out. "Figured I was in the neighborhood, I'd let you in on the secret."

She scanned it briefly, handed it back. "Hmmm. Been a whole year, huh? Time passes quickly, when you're up to your ass in blood."

Scully appraised her gory OR scrubs. "You wear it well, Ma'am, if I do say so myself."

"'Ma'am', my ass. Brown-noser."

She started toward the mess hall, the clerk bobbing along at her side. He said, "I've got a little ceremony of my own coming up, you know."

"You're out of here next month, right? Good for you."

Scully gave her the private-punch-line grin. "Actually, Ma'am, that's not exactly the case."

The Lieutenant halted and glared at him. "Oh, Christ—you *didn't*."

His grin grew to Cheshire Cat proportions.

"Scully—how *could* you? You, of all people." Scully was beyond irreverent, his sense of humor sick even by Viet Nam standards. She had seen his corner of the Enlisted Men's hooch in Phu Bai: his cot had been covered with a Confederate flag, and his piece of the wall studded with the mummified bodies of poison-skinned toads. There were 18 of them, he'd bragged. He had hunted them down in the latrine and stabbed them with pencils, then pounded the pencils into the room's plywood walls.

She gave him a suspicious look. "You're pulling my leg here, right? You didn't re-up."

"I most certainly did. I signed on the dotted line just this morning."

"You twisted fuck." She threw out a gesture that took in the compound—the Quonsets baking in the hard mid-day sun; the grass-less grounds; the boxy two-story Officers' Quarters. "Why would anyone want to stay in this shithole for a whole extra year?"

"Perquisites," said Scully.

"PERquisites? What—mortar shells, malaria, a day off every week to go to the massage parlor and get the clap? Not to mention all the shit you can eat from the guys with the bars and eagles and stars? Bullshit. You can work in a nice, air-conditioned office in the *real* world and get all the perquisites you want. *real* perquisites!"

"Tsk, tsk, tsk. How you do take on, Lieutenant."

She stared at him, exasperated. "This isn't the Scully I know and revile."

"The truth, Lieutenant? I'm a *clerk*." He shrugged. "What'm I gonna do back in the World? Be somebody's receptionist?" He lifted a mock phone receiver to his ear. "'Mr. Shitzowski can't see you right now, Mrs. Shitzowski—he's busy porkin' his secretary.'" He barked a laugh. "See, Lieutenant, you-all get the crap, you nurses and techs. Me, I get respect. Not to mention a tidy little re-up bonus and a sergeant's stripe. Give me a couple hitches, I'll rule the world."

"Machiavellian asshole." She sighed. "Well, congratulations. I guess."

"You, too—*First* Lieutenant." He snapped her a smart salute.

She again lifted a finger. "Get real, *Sergeant* Scully."

The Lieutenant thought about Scully as she ate her lunch of beef stew with canned gravy and drank her filled milk. As much as she hated to admit it, she could see the little weasel's point. Even she, as a nurse, received a measure of respect here that she would never have achieved at home. Back in the States, she would be meekly handing instruments to surgeons, playing whipping-boy when their stress levels hit overload. She would be paid shit. She would be hit upon by men simply because she was a nurse and—as a blind date had once told her—"nurses are easy; they know it all."

Here, she clipped and stitched like a surgeon herself. Doctors seldom bitched at her unjustly—she was a vital team member, and they knew it. Her pay, while nothing to crow about, was the same that men of her rank received. And, given the female-to-male ratio, men treated her with a regard that bordered on reverence.

Still, you'd never see her sign up for extra time. Not here. Not in the Army. The Lieutenant forked up a soggy potato, two grey peas gravy-glued to it like eyes. In her humble opinion, even respect took a back seat to basic morality.

The Lieutenant received her automatic promotion two days later, as predicted. It was a low-key ritual. A general pinned the silver bar on the collar of her fatigue shirt, over her yellow second lieutenant's patch, and moved on to the next honoree.

The general was tall and gaunt, with hands that trembled and a bald head flecked with moles and sweat. She didn't know him personally. Perhaps he was the hospital CO; she been in Chu Lai less than a month, and had yet to meet the local high command. Or maybe he was someone farther up the food chain. There were a number of High Brass in town at the moment; it seemed her little ceremony had coincided with something grander, some prestigious unit citation about which the Lieutenant knew nothing. Just that morning, she had seen a raft of colonels and generals wandering the hospital grounds. The Lieutenant had been relieved to hear that these intimidating old farts were not billeted at the hospital, but rather in more luxurious quarters on the nearby Americal compound.

They were, however, eating at least one meal here. The Lieutenant discovered this when she dropped by the mess hall for a snack that evening, after her shift.

The entrance was draped with bunting. The Lieutenant stood beneath it and watched, fascinated, as Scully strutted back and forth with a clipboard, supervising a half-dozen mama-sans who hung balloons and streamers from the rafters. The long tables were covered in white and crowned with luxuriant bouquets of local flowers.

The Lieutenant moved inside, a blood-stained Alice stepping through the looking glass. She touched a tabletop: real cloth.

At the rear, in front of the now-bare cafeteria serving lineup, a cloth-covered table groaned under metal washtubs heaped with ice. Two women stood behind it. They were tall young beauties, expertly made up, manicured, and coifed, elegantly slender in floor-length evening gowns and long white gloves. One was white; the other was a light-skinned, fine-featured black woman. They held their heads high, their backs as straight and regal as princesses', and surveyed the room with a charming shared indifference. *Salt and pepper thoroughbreds*, the Lieutenant thought. Europeans; models, perhaps, or actresses.

It had been more than four months since the Lieutenant had seen women dressed for a real party. She felt drawn to them, enchanted by their perfection; she moved between the festive tables, past the clerk and his clipboard, past a mama-san curling red, white and blue crepe-paper. An old papa-san brushed by her, and dumped a load of boiled shrimp on the ice.

The black woman picked up a shrimp that had dropped to the table and placed it back on the pile, then brushed her gloved fingers together. She glanced up at the Lieutenant and gave her a slight, flawless red curve of a smile.

The Lieutenant smiled in return. "Hi—I was just wondering what was going on here," she said.

The woman's smile faltered.

"I mean," said the Lieutenant, "You guys look great. You must've come a long way for this; must be some important deal—"

The black woman looked down. She shook her head, turned to her companion, spoke. In Vietnamese.

"Hey, Lieutenant—how's about a shrimp?" Scully's voice at her back. She turned. Her pleasantries hung in the air like cartoon balloons; she felt awkward, embarrassed, as if she'd been caught at something shady.

"Me, I don't care much for shrimp, myself," the clerk said. "Reminds me of big bugs." He nodded his head toward a burst of bunting above them. "Whaddya think?"

"You've become an interior decorator. How very chic."

"Yeah. 'Not there, Marybelle,'" he lisped to an imaginary worker, flapping his wrist. "'Over the verAHNda!'" He brandished the clipboard. "They know me better than that—they got it all spelled out, with maps and diagrams and all."

The Lieutenant glanced back at the two women, her salt-and-pepper thoroughbreds. "And who are they?"

"Ah. Those young ladies came up special delivery from Saigon." He winked lasciviously.

The Lieutenant's enchantment dissolved. "You mean, they're just—"

"Call them decorations. Not bad, huh? French daddies, I'd say."

"Perquisites."

"You might say that." Scully grinned. "The generals wanted to invite you nurses, but the logistics were too tough."

The Lieutenant threw him a withering glance. "So they got a couple of call girls instead. Thanks a *lot*. That's pretty damned crass, Scully. Even for you."

He shrugged. "You think I'm kidding? The paperwork requested you-all. But there's too many nurses here, and they'd take up too much space. Some two-star from HQ asked me if he might come through and pick out certain ones—but his aide convinced him that that just might be viewed as undemocratic. Of course, the Light Colonel and the Major get to come, but you can bet your ass they ain't who the generals want to rub—uh—shoulders with."

She thought of the gaunt general with the speckled head and shaking hands, and her stomach sank.

Scully pulled a pack of cigarettes from his pocket and held it out. "You still don't indulge?"

She shook her head and sank onto a folding chair.

"Hell," he said, shaking the match out, "even generals need some loving every once in a while. Tough bird like you, Lieutenant, you surely do understand the facts of life." He sucked in smoke, blew it out. "How 'bout that shrimp? You want, I can hustle you up a plate."

The Lieutenant glanced at the table, but saw the women behind it. Her stomach churned; she loved shrimp, but she had suddenly lost her appetite. She shook her head.

Scully peered at her quizzically through his smoke. "You okay, Lieutenant?"

She glanced up at him and forced a smile. "Sure. Tough bird like me, why wouldn't I be?"

Broken Stone

"I'm—ah—sorry. It's my—" He grimaced.

Diane Zytch raised her head; the tips of her hair drifted lightly over his chin. He freed up his right hand and brushed at it.

"Sorry. It itches, you know."

"That's two sorries." She touched her finger to his nose. "It's your *what*?"

He could feel himself blush; he wondered if she could see it in the meager candlelight. He shifted his body slightly under her. "I just—well, I'm sorry—"

She raised a feathery eyebrow. The hair swept down, now over his nose, while her finger traced his thin upper lip.

"It's my first time." He closed his eyes. "This is hard."

"It's okay." She removed her hand and placed it beside him, then leaned her weight to her elbow. "That's sweet, Devvy. We all have a first time. Why is that hard?"

He shifted again. "No, I mean *this*." He dropped his hand on the hardness beneath them, beneath the skewed white cloth; the blow sent a ripple through their bodies, trembling the soft flesh of her breasts where they rested lightly against him. "*This* is hard. Maybe we should—get up or something?"

She settled her weight back upon him gently, more firmly. "Let's try again, huh? Then it won't be your first time." She moved softly. "What do you think, huh?"

He brushed her hair out of his mouth; it caught the guttery light like spider webbing. He'd noticed her hair right off, the first time he'd seen her in the mess hall, the very day he'd come to work here in Chu Lai some six months ago. White-blond, unapologetic dark roots.

Trashy; sexy. Forbidden. He felt himself stir between her legs, and moved his hand down to her bottom. Funny, how she looked plump and loose, almost a little fat. But she felt compact, smooth, round—

Pain ground through his lower spine, brought him back. He wondered, dimly, if it was because the vodka was wearing off.

"Ummm," she said. "That's right...."

"Uh—Diane. Maybe we could move—maybe even the floor, if I—"

"Oooo—yeah. Like that." She shifted again, caught him. "That's it—"

It felt marvelous. It felt horrible. He wanted to pull out, he wanted to go *in*—

But he couldn't go anywhere on his own—his back was pinned, *crushed*, and she was moving now, and he didn't have to do anything, really, but arch his buttocks a bit if he could, when he could—

He could. He could. He could—it was coming like an effing *train*, pulling him up by the roots, the *root*—

Devon Conlon pulled his mind down desperately, pulled his eyes open, pulled his brain back, back, back—bases loaded, he thought frantically, *threeballstwostrikes*—no good; his entire body was being sucked into her slippery, delicious—he cast about valiantly for something to hook himself onto, to dig into, to hold, and his eyes caught the crucifix on the wall behind and above them, but—

He felt himself slide and—

"Pray!" she said feverishly. "Jesus fucking Christ, *pray*!"

He gasped—"Ahh—*ahhhgnus* Dei!"

"That's good, that's *good*," she panted. "More! *Pray*!"

"*Qui tollis pe-caaaa*—" He gritted his teeth—"*mundi*—" He wrenched his eyes open, stared at the cross, at the little metal toes of the corpus twinkling in the candle flames, the little metal nail above them.

"Ah! Ah!" she cried. "Mooooore..."

"*Miserere*—"

He lost his grip, lost himself; the crucifix swam away, and he exploded—"*Nobis*!!"—in waves of bright ecstasy and, beneath it, sharpening pain at the dig of her hips and the kink of his spine into the hard, creaking planks of the Hospital Chapel altar.

Everything went still. She sighed deeply and propped herself again on one elbow, pulling a sweat-sticky breast free. It made a sound like peeling off a big bandaid. "Better?"

"Did you—"

She wiped at her brow with the back of her wrist. "I'm okay. You did okay."

His back felt as if it'd been mashed beneath a pile of sandbags. He gathered his muscles, then pushed himself against the bulk of her. She gave way slowly, indolently rolled to the side, casually reached a leg down until her foot touched the floor.

"Ah, Jeez—" He sat up, pushing her onto her other foot. "Ah, jeez. Ah, *Jeez*!" She padded away, and he picked the starched cloth from the crack of his ass, then leapt to his feet. He smoothed at the white altar cloth; it was bunched up in sharp wrinkles and at its center, his palm met a large, warm, sticky-wet spot. "Ah, jeez, Diane—"

In the shadows beyond him, a lighter flared and lit her face for an instant, then all was dark except for the bright pinpoint of light that was the tip of her cigarette. He hauled the cloth from the altar and over to one of the two side candles she'd lit a half-hour ago, a world ago, when this had seemed like such an urgent and daring and, yes, *hilarious* idea. He held it up: there was no blood—not that he expected it from her, but who knows, maybe from him? Just a large, amorphous spot, translucent in its wet glory.

His stomach roiled slightly. What would he say to the mama-san who did the laundry? He sent up a silent prayer of thanks for that small pile of crisp altar linen that he knew lay in the little makeshift sacristy of this little makeshift church.

He draped the cloth back over the altar, smoothing it absently, and glanced in her direction. "Diane?"

A long exhalation. "Yeah?"

"I...wish you wouldn't smoke in here."

A snort of laughter, deep and throaty; the light speck intensified, then dimmed. Fine tendrils of smoke drifted toward him, caught the flickering candle light. "Did you really say that?"

He leaned against the side of the altar. "I don't think that's unreasonable."

She chuckled richly and said nothing.

"This is—" He rubbed at his mangled sacrum with his thumb— "This was a little...strange, don't you think?"

The cigarette point brightened, dimmed. A pause. "Was it?"

"Well, yes."

She said nothing.

"You know. Doing *it*. Here."

Nothing. Then, "Did I kidnap you?"

He leaned forward and squinted. She was planted in the aisle, on the floor, a rounded shadow against the first folding chair in the first row. "No." His voice felt rusty. "But I was, I don't know... I had all that booze, and you were so—" He cleared his throat. "So—I don't know—insistent? So—" He stared into the gloom, trying to see her face, to distinguish it from the bulk of her.

"Did you enjoy it?"

"Well, yes. I enjoyed it. Of course I enjoyed it." And he did. Yes, he did—but as he looked out from the spot where Father LeMieux stood on Sundays, out at the darkness that he knew contained chairs— right there—and, there, a stack of missals for his Catholics, and over there, on the side, hymnbooks for the Protestants, the giddiness was gone, and he felt the pull of something dark, regretful. Something he had felt as a child when he'd screwed up royally, and his mother didn't know. Yet.

He felt guilt.

She rose slowly, stretching. The candlelight shaped the soft folds of her skin, a lighter dark against black. She walked toward him;

more and more of her emerging, an idea becoming flesh, round hips, belly. Ah jeez, she was amazing. Her body was. He felt himself aroused and ashamed and fascinated. He fought the urge to reach out to her.

She crossed her arms beneath those marvelous breasts and looked him in the eyes. "I always wanted to seduce a priest," she said lightly.

"I'm not a priest."

"Failing that, I wanted to fuck an altar boy." She brought the cigarette to her mouth and took a drag.

"I'm not an altar boy."

"I bet you were."

"Sure. Every Catholic boy was."

"So what else is a chaplain's assistant, except a glorified altar boy. No pun intended."

"Huh?"

"The 'glorified' part."

"Oh. Very funny." He touched the cloth on the altar again, smoothing it with his palm.

Again, the throaty laugh.

He bristled. "What's so funny?"

"I dunno." She sucked briefly on the cigarette, then dropped the butt on the floor, moved her heel toward it, pulled back—her foot was bare. "I just think of you, trying to tell this in confession. 'Father, I told a lie, and I read two girlie magazines. Oh—and I fucked an officer on the altar.'"

Devon Conlon reached down and picked up the glowing butt, held it away from him. What could he do with this? It wasn't as if they had ashtrays in the chapel. He turned it gingerly in his fingers, wondering if he should feel different, physically, now—more complicated. More wise. Wondering why he only felt confused, slightly nauseated. And sore.

She turned and walked back to the first row and sat down. A sigh from the darkness. Then, "You know who I really, really always wanted to fuck? As a kid?"

"I don't know." He squatted down and shoved the head of the cigarette against the wood floor until the glow went out. As he stood up, it dropped from his fingers. He looked down, but the candles were high; their light didn't reach the floor. A feeling of panic rose in his belly; he considered switching on the overhead light, then dismissed the idea with a shudder. What if someone saw it through a crack in the curtains and came in? It was past midnight, but people stayed up 'til all hours here; it was a hospital, after all. Ah, jeez.

"'My guardian angel has erased the board for me,'" she said in a mock-deep voice. "What're you doing over there, all that thrashing around?"

"I'm looking for my pants. I don't remember where I put my pants."

"I've got your shirt here." She tossed his fatigue shirt forward, and it landed in a pool of shadow at the foot of the altar. "Your pants are over in the corner, I think. The angel and the blackboard—remember?"

He felt the floor in the darkness with his feet and produced a pair of fatigue pants, picked them up. "Bishop Fulton J. Sheen," he said. They were hers. He dropped them and felt around again, this time with his hands.

"Aha—you watched him too. I always thought he was cute. Great eyes. Good sense of humor. A little corny—but he couldn't exactly tell dirty jokes on TV." She rose and moved to the altar, pulled the cloth off and held it up in his direction. "Just wrap this around you, why don't you?"

Another pair of pants; these were his. He draped them around his neck. Now, where were his boxers?

"No? Okay then, I'll use it."

He glanced up and saw her standing in the candlelight, wrapped in the cloth. The sight alarmed him—the more so, because it titillated him. He stepped up to her. "Very funny," he said, and took it from her, averting his eyes from her naked body. Carefully, he spread the cloth on the altar once again. Thank God for tropical heat; it had already begun to dry. But the spot was hardening; from what he could see, it was also darkening.

"It's only a tablecloth, Dev. What's the big deal?"

He shuffled back toward where he'd found his pants, feeling the floor with his feet. "The big deal is–" Ah–his boxers–"it's–*you* know what it is. All this stuff." He pulled the shorts on. "What've you got against sacred things?"

She disappeared into the shadows, lit another cigarette. "Devvy, my little Altar Boy," she sucked in, exhaled. "You've been here, what–six months? Isn't that long enough to know that *nothing* is sacred?"

"To you." He said it very softly, surprised at the bitter taste of the words.

"What was that?"

"Nothing."

"C'mon, Dev." She drew smoke in, spoke through it. "What'd you say?"

"I said, 'To you.' Nothing is sacred to you." Now, he actually felt low, bummed. In spite of the heat, his body was cold. He stuck a foot into his pants, but the leg was pulled through the wrong way. He righted it, irritated–he had been in such a hurry–

"I suppose that's true." Once again, the laugh–low, ironic. "Hey–wanna hear a joke? Did you know, when I came here ten months ago, I was a virgin?"

His head snapped up, and he squinted in her direction, a combat boot clutched in both hands. "No."

"Ah, yes. Not only that, I believed in–" The glowing cigarette tip waved grandly–"all this. You know? All this. Not just the religion thing. Everything. The war, My Country, Right or Wrong. All this."

"And?"

She coughed gently. "It's not important."

He walked to where she sat and lowered himself onto the chair next to hers, still holding the boot. She was so close; he could see her now, dimly, a ghost in the dark. The shadowed hollows of her eyes, the upturned tilt of her nose, the smooth hint of lightness that was her hair; it touched him with a strange tenderness. "No, Diane. I'm listening. What happened?"

She smoked thoughtfully for a moment. "I don't know how you can be—here—and ask that."

He tugged the boot onto his foot. "I don't question faith. You can't question faith. That's why it's faith. Here or anywhere."

She took a drag on the cigarette. "Doesn't your faith say that God decides who will live and who will die?"

"Well—sort of—"

"The sparrows, right? The hairs on your heads are numbered, all that shit?"

"I—"

"Look at me. You're looking at God." She flung the cigarette on the floor. "I'm God. When I'm in Triage, that's me—God. I get to say who lives and who dies."

He steeled himself to keep from rising to find the cigarette butt. "That's not the way it works."

"Yeah. Tell that to some poor bastard who's lost his whole lower half, when he looks up at you and says, 'I'm going to make it, right?' and you're the one—shit—that makes sure he doesn't. Or a guy with burns all over him—"

He reached out his hand; it hovered over her thigh for an instant, then he pulled it back. "Sometimes, things just happen. That doesn't mean God isn't watching. That doesn't mean you don't need faith."

"And he's on our side, this God, right?" She leaned back on her chair.

"He doesn't take sides. I mean—" Devon's head had begun to ache; he massaged his right temple with his fingers. "You just can't pin Him down like that."

"How about 'Thou shalt not kill?' He pinned himself down on that one, didn't he?"

"There are, you know. Extenuating circumstances."

Diane Zytch rose heavily; he could hear, rather than see, that she was pulling her shirt on. "Sure," she said. "There always are."

"You're bitter."

"I'm not. I'm not bitter."

"Yes, you are. Consider what you—what we've just done." He stood and glanced about. "We have, at your behest—and it really *was* your idea, you can't deny it—desecrated a church. Where'd you throw my shirt?"

"Down there." She pointed, the nail of her index finger twinkling briefly. "Right below the scene of the crime. Beneath the carved marble of the sacred sacrificial altar, the most sacred point of this vast and beautiful cathedral you're so eager to protect from the likes of me."

One foot still bare, he clumped to the altar. "Maybe it's not a cathedral, but it's as close as we've got here to a real church."

She sighed. "Look, Dev. I don't want to argue with you. It's late; we're both tired, and arguing religion is just fucking impossible, because no one ever wants to give an inch. I know; I've been on the other side. Arguing for my good old Catholic beliefs in my public high school. But there's something you don't get about me. About this." She stepped to the altar, leaned against it, watched him button his shirt. Then she said, "I did it as a consecration, if you really want to know."

"I beg your pardon?"

"What we did. Fucking on the altar. It wasn't a desecration at all. It was a consecration. Or maybe even a purification."

He looked at her, shaking his head. "You're out of your mind."

"No." Her face was earnest. "I'm *right*, is what I am. We consecrated this sorry slab of wood, this converted card table. What we did, Dev, was about life. That's why I wanted to do it so badly."

"Give me a break."

"Think about it."

"It's beyond me." He unfastened the shirt—it was off by one button—and carefully set it straight.

"What we're living in—here, in this country, in this war—that's all about death. And sin—real sin. Killing. Raping. Stealing. Hating. Jesus Christ—it's about just about every sin in the commandments, except maybe honoring your father and mother. And if God goes along with it, he's just not any kind of god that we should be dealing with. He can't be. Just like he can't be against fucking, because it's love. And God, God *himself*, is love, right? So He can't be against what we did—"

"Now you sound like one of those hippies. 'God is Love—so let's make love! Free love—the answer to everything. Make love, not war!' Give me a break."

"Maybe they're right. Maybe they're right about all that."

He snorted. "They're a bunch of free-loading, dirty kids. Pretty pathetic, if you ask me."

"I don't remember you complaining about Free Love when you were ripping off my clothes."

"You're nuts. Really, you're nuts."

"I might be." She walked behind the altar and, after some searching, located her fatigue pants and his second boot. "But I'd rather be my kind of nuts than yours. I feel sorry for you, you know? 'Waking alone at an hour when we are trembling with tenderness, lips that would kiss form prayers to broken stone.' That's you. I give you something tender—I give you myself? And you're just worrying about how you're going to clean up my fucking cigarette butts after I leave."

He stood, hand gripping the altar's edge, face clenched. "You can quote Shakespeare at me all you want, but in the end, it doesn't make any difference. None of this does. None of this—what you say— matters." He felt a rush of anger; a physical, violent anger; a fury. Part of him, a cool and separate him, marveled at this, noted that it was completely out of proportion to this discussion, to them. He squared his jaw, closed his eyes, reined his heartbeat, forced himself to breathe deeply once, twice. Control.

When he spoke again, his voice was, he thought, admirably smooth. Quiet. Logical. "God isn't for you or me to decide about, Diane. He's just *there*, and either you accept Him on faith, mysteries and all, or you don't—and you go to Hell. Which makes me feel sorry for *you*."

She pulled on her pants. She walked to him and handed him his combat boot, her hand lingering on it after he had taken it, her eyes on his. His anger seeped away; he gripped the leather with both hands to keep from reaching out, touching her, putting his arms around her. In spite of the make-up, the hair roots, the booze, the cigarettes, her round face held a puzzling serenity, almost an innocence.

"It's Eliot," she said softly.

"What's Eliot?"

"About the broken stone. That's from T.S. Eliot, the same poem about the world ending not with a bang, but with a whimper." Her smile was quick and tight. "Doesn't fit your neat little image of me, does it. Sluts don't read poetry, right?" She stood on tiptoe and kissed him lightly on the tip of his nose. "Maybe I'm one of those mysteries; maybe you don't have the faith to handle me. Bye, bye, Altar Boy." She stepped back and winked. "See you in Hell."

And she was gone.

Devon Conlon picked a candle from its simple gold-plated holder and held it up to light his way into the modified walk-in closet that served as sacristy. He pulled a clean altar cloth from the mama-san's stack and grabbed two new candles. He would replace the melted stubs, find the butts, burn the evidence. Or bury it. He would re-create order; everything in its place. It could be done; there was time.

He stuck the candle back in its holder and balled up the soiled cloth. He glanced around the room. He brought the white bundle to his nose.

She was there

Monkey on our Backs

The day she hacked her braid off, Keeler vowed that the Major's monkey had to die.

The monkey had been passed down to the Major by another nurse, a captain, who'd left Viet Nam the year before. It had been given to the captain by a surgeon who had reduced a fracture in its femur. It had been brought to the surgeon by a mama-san whose job it had been to scrub the surgeon's fatigues. It had come to the mama-san, it was said, from the family of a Chinese merchant who had sold joss sticks and red envelopes for Tet; the merchant himself had been killed in an explosion that had destroyed his shop and broken the monkey's leg.

The monkey had been acquired by the merchant, it was presumed, from some anonymous soul who had captured it in the jungle.

But the monkey's checkered past was beside the point for Keeler, as she scissored at the fat auburn rope that had been her pride for so many years. The point was that the Major's monkey was at the moment positively thriving, as were the vermin that lived in its coat.

For a week, Keeler had scrubbed her head with tar shampoo. For a week, she had snagged at her hair-roots with a nit comb. Still, the Major's monkey's lively lice frolicked through her waist-length tresses and set her scalp on fire.

So—desperate, despairing—she clipped away eight years' growth of hair. Her reflection streamed and melted in her little mirror, and her soul turned to ice.

The Major's monkey had to die.

There were so Very Many Reasons, even beyond the cooties. *Clip.* It lay in wait in the darkness, leapt on Keeler, scared the living shit out of her. *Clip.* It was nauseatingly flatulent. *Clip.* It looted and vandalized. *Clip.* It was a flea-and-louse-ridden, devious, farting, plundering demon, and it had, for reasons known to God alone, targeted her.

CLIP.

Complaining to the Major was futile—*Can you prove little Sage ate your candy bars?*

Prove it? Chocolate hand-ish footprints, wrapper shreds, a disoriented flea foundering on the bed, the stench of monkey-farts. But the Major's love was blind, deaf, dumb and possessed of a lousy sense of smell. She merely shrugged her shoulder—the one without Sage's furry ass on it—and said, *That could've been anyone. It* wasn't *my Little Wise Man.*

Whatever a major told a lieutenant was Truth Inviolable. And there was no appealing to the Head Nurse; the Lieutenant-Colonel was the Major's best friend.

Keeler threw the mirror a last teary glance and grabbed her tar shampoo.

As she grimly scoured her head under the shower—cold again, in spite of the ministrations of those robotic little repairmen from Philco Ford—she pondered the greatest mystery of all: she had never seen the Major scratch. Never. Could you selectively infect people? Could you ignore a friend and aim lice at a foe?

The Major's monkey had to die. Keeler was a nurse, a Saver of Lives. She was not a killer. Even after all she'd been through, she wasn't bold, cold-blooded, crazy, or—quite possibly—strong enough to kill the thing herself.

But she knew someone who would be perfect for the job.

* * *

"Let me get this straight." The Marine swirled the scotch in his glass. "You want me to kill a monkey."

"Shh." Keeler glanced around the club. Two guys played pool in the corner, a lone captain slumped at the bar, and the bartender absently polished a glass and stared out the picture window at the night-black South China Sea. She turned back to the Marine. "Yes."

"Why?"

She leaned forward, arms on the table, voice low and vehement. "Because I hate the monkey."

He grinned. "You said you hated me. But you never swore a contract out on me."

"God knows, I considered it. You could be such a bastard. Which reminds me—how's your wife?"

"Ow." He gulped his drink. "Direct hit." He lifted his empty glass, but failed to catch the bartender's eye. "I never understood your problem, Keeler. You didn't seem to mind my—ah—methods. And I wouldn't be half as good without regular practice."

"I had a good time, Ollie. I just don't like being lied to."

"Big morals, for someone who wants to murder a monkey."

She stirred her gin and tonic. "That's funny, Ollie."

"Thanks. So. Tell me more."

Keeler told him about the Major's monkey. About pilfered Clark Bars—the real thing, real chocolate, not the powdery tropical shit. About gnawed electrical cords. Ravaged lace undies. Desecrated bedding. And about the lice.

The Marine gave a low whistle. "He gave you *crabs*?"

The captain at the bar swiveled on his stool.

"Shhhh! Not *crabs*, you ass. *Head* lice."

"Crabs is crabs. So that's why the...hair, huh?"

She tugged at a lock. "Do you think I'd do something like this on a whim?"

"Hey. I think it looks good. Different. Kind of...sexy."

"Right."

His eyes gleamed. "I got crabs once from some broad. Got rid of 'em in one night—sprayed Raid on my pecker. Hurt like a sonovabitch, but damn, it did the trick. See, I really am a nice guy. Gave you my secret. For free."

She stirred her drink grimly.

He raised his glass again; this time, the bartender nodded. "Why don't you just lock your hooch? You always locked your hooch when I was there."

"I *latched* it. You can only latch a door from the inside."

"Good thing nobody steals things in the Army."

"We padlock our valuables in our footlockers."

"Your Clark Bars aren't valuable?"

"My Clark Bars are gold. But I'd just gotten the Care Package, and I had all my pizza mixes in my footlocker."

"So how'd you know it was the monkey?"

She buried her face in her hands. "Trust me, you don't have to be Sherlock Holmes to know it was the monkey."

He pulled a package of Camels from his pocket and offered her one.

She shook her head.

He raised an eyebrow. "Sure?"

"I quit. A week ago."

"Again?"

"Leave me alone. With all this stress, it's killing me to turn that down. I need support, not flak."

The Marine lit up. "If you need support, get a bra. This monkey: does he bite?"

"He's never bit me, but he took a chunk out of the Major's ex-boyfriend. He had to have stitches."

"Which would explain why he's an EX-boyfriend."

The bartender materialized with a bottle of Chivas and refilled the Marine's glass. The Marine exhaled a stream of smoke. "So. How're you going to catch it?"

Keeler's eyes widened. "Me? Catch it?"

"Somebody has to catch it, if I'm gonna kill it. Which is a

hypothetical *if,* given that we haven't established what's in it for me."
He winked.

"Can't you catch it?"

"Yeah. Sure. I sneak past the guard, hang around your hooch, grab the little fucker. Stick him in a sack and cart him off. Smooth. Who'd notice a guy dragging a sack full of monkey out of a woman's hooch?"

"Okay, okay. Point taken." She stirred the gin and tonic. In spite of the club's grinding air conditioner, the ice had disappeared. "I'll catch him. Somehow. Then, *you'll* kill him, right?"

"You know, contrary to popular belief, I don't go around killing animals for the hell of it."

"You've killed *people* for the hell of it. Or so you say. Or was that a lie, too?"

"Not people. Gooks. There's a difference."

She sighed heavily. "Damn it, Ollie, you owe me. If not for the lies, for that jeep."

He tapped his cigarette ash on the floor. "Jeep."

"The *hospital* jeep. I put my butt on the line for you."

He held up a hand. "Okay, okay—enough. I'm a bastard. But nobody says I don't repay my debts."

She smiled tightly. "Okay. I'll call you when I've got him. Deal?"

He stuck the Camel in the corner of his mouth and snapped a salute. "Deal, *Sir.*"

She drank deeply.

He said, "You know, I think I can find a good use for your monkey."

"He's not my monkey; he's all yours. Do what you want. *Marry* the little creep, if you want." She slapped her forehead. "Silly me. You're *already* married."

"Ow." He gulped his scotch. "Direct hit."

* * *

At lunch time the next day, Keeler walked casually to her hooch, her heart pounding in her throat. *What if he didn't come? What if he came, ate, and fell asleep somewhere else?*

She opened her door carefully.

God, oh God—there is a God.

The monkey lay sprawled on her bed, atop her poncho liner. Asleep, chest rising and falling, beard matted with tomato sauce and pizza crumbs. She tiptoed closer, bent over him; his hairy belly hitched and he let fly an effortless fart.

"Jesus!"

She grabbed the corrugated cardboard box that had once held her books. This could be tricky; she didn't know how long the Librium would last. *Maybe I should've asked for Valium*, she thought, pulling the sleep-heavy body into the box.

She taped the lid shut, re-taped it, inspected it, taped it again, then—*what the hell*—poked her pen through the side twice for ventilation.

Now—to call Ollie.

She hesitated. What if he wasn't home? What if he got here, and the monkey woke up?

She opened the door and glanced out into the compound. Her eyes lit upon a small man, a Korean man in a baseball cap who stood, wrench in hand, at the shower house door.

Philco Ford.

Thank you, God. "Excuse me?" she called. "Sir?"

The man looked up.

She stepped into the sunshine. "I have a favor to ask."

The man walked over.

She smiled. "Can you," she spoke slowly, "do something for me?"

He cocked his head.

"I need to send a box to MAG 13." Slowly; distinctly. "To the beach."

He nodded.

"I will pay you." She pulled a ten-dollar MPC note from her pocket.

The man nodded.

"In here." She held the screened door open. The man hesitated, then walked inside.

Her heart hammered as he sized up the box. "To who, lady?" He rolled the "*l*" into a near "*r*."

"Oh. Hold on." She snatched a pen from the bedside table, flicking away a pizza crumb, and wrote the Marine's name on the box.

The man hoisted the box—*Did the load shift?* "It's books," Keeler said quickly. "Just *books*. You can leave them at the MAG 13 USO."

He cocked his head.

"At the *U-S-O*," she repeated loudly.

The man nodded. He paused expectantly.

"Oh. Sorry." She stuffed the MPC bill in his shirt pocket.

As he carried the box to his jeep, Keeler congratulated herself. Nobody would question a Philco Ford worker with a cardboard box. Philco Ford workers always wandered around with cardboard boxes.

*   *   *

Sage awoke dizzy and supremely hungry. He grasped the rim of the box and pulled himself to his feet. The box yawed, flopped forward, pitched him face-down on the ground.

Laughter. "Jesus, would you looka that!"

"Looks like he's drunk."

Marines. Everywhere. Watching him. Sage smelled something tangy; his stomach growled.

Scattered before the men were mess kits and opened cans.

Sage righted himself. He grinned, stretching his upper lip, and wobbled to the nearest man.

The marine grinned back. He held out a piece of baloney.

Sage snatched it and crammed it in his mouth. Something hit his flank; he looked down, saw a little brown glob. He picked it up, sniffed, gobbled it down.

Thump. Thump. Thump. Laughter. He was pelted with food. He dropped to the ground, blinked twice, and scooped the goodies out of the dust.

* * *

At nine p.m., Keeler heard a knock at her door. She lay atop her poncho liner, which she had shaken out, fumigated and reversed. Keeler was feeling out-of-sorts. After work, she'd passed the Major in the compound.

The Major had been weeping, leaning against her best friend, the Lieutenant-Colonel, the Head Nurse.

"There, there," the Lieutenant-Colonel had said. "We'll find your little Sage. There, there."

Keeler hated feeling out-of-sorts. She told herself it was the letdown after this noon's adventure. But she knew better: Keeler had grown up Catholic. She could recognize guilt.

So, when she dragged herself to the door of her hooch, when she opened it, she was only vaguely surprised to see the little Korean man from Philco Ford.

He eyed her sternly from beneath his baseball cap. "I know," he said.

"Excuse me?"

"Come," he said.

As if compelled, she slipped out the door.

The man led her to his jeep. He pointed to the passenger seat.

Keeler balked. "What do you want?"

"I know." He scratched his sides with both hands.

Like a monkey.

Sweat trickled into the bra beneath her shirt. She craved a cigarette. "Shit," she said quietly.

"*I know.*"

She swallowed. "Okay," she said. "You know. So what do you want from me?"

"Come." he said. "Eat."

Her jaw dropped. "Eat? You want a date with me?"

He nodded.

"That's it—just to eat?"

He nodded.

"And you won't—"

"No tell Major." He rolled the "*r*" into a near "*l.*"

Keeler climbed into the jeep. "This just gets curiouser and curiouser," she said under her breath.

* * *

"Shoot it."

The New Guy shook his buzz-cut head.

"Shoot the fucking thing." The sergeant spoke softly. "You wanted to know if you could—what'd you say? 'Overcome your moral im-PER-tives and kill a man?'"

"Imperatives," mumbled the New Guy.

"You coRECTing me, boy?"

"No, sir." The New Guy's sweaty, knuckly hand slipped on the barrel of the M-16. He stared at the monkey tethered to the slender tree.

The monkey stared at him. Its old man face held a severe wisdom. As if it had suffered. As if it understood.

"Look, F-N-G." The sergeant leaned into the New Guy, crowded him with muscle, sweat, fetid breath. "If you can't shoot a fucking *monkey*, how the fuck to you expect to shoot a fucking *Gook*?"

"I—I don't know, sir."

"'I I don't know, Sir,'" the sergeant mimicked. "You don't know jack *shit*, F-N-G." He jabbed a fat finger into the New Guy's chest with each letter. "You got no balls. All you got's a moral im-PER-tive." *Jab, Jab, Jab*. "And a moral im-PER-tive ain't gonna save your ass out there. Am I right, gentlemen?"

Heads nodded. "Yep." "Right on." "You betcha, Sarge."

"So I suggest," the Sergeant said conversationally, "You shoot that fucking monkey."

The New Guy raised the M-16. It was heavy as a corpse.

Someone coughed; someone tittered.

The sergeant watched through slitted eyes.

The New Guy swallowed and aimed. The monkey stood, eyes inscrutable, humanoid hands clutching the rope at its neck, a rope tied to the tree behind it.

The New Guy took a deep breath, squeezed his eyes shut.

The monkey blinked twice.

The M16 fired, shattering the forest.

Silence.

Then: laughter. The New Guy opened his eyes, looked around, dazed.

The sergeant squatted, holding his stomach. Heaving with laughter.

The men sat in the dust, howling with laughter.

The New Guy's face flushed, anger flooding every freckle. He lowered the M-16 and glared at the sergeant.

"Jesus Fucking Christ," the sergeant gasped. "Fucking monkey's smarter than you, F-N-G."

"You had no right to make me do that." The New Guy's voice was high, thin as a blade.

The sergeant roared anew.

"You made me kill an innocent—" The New Guy's words

tangled, clogged in his throat.

Hot, humiliating moments hitched by, rough-rode the sergeant's merry hiccoughs.

At last, tears streaming, the sergeant wheezed, "You didn't kill *nothing*, F-N-G. Except–except maybe that–sorry-assed f-fucking–– hic–*tree*."

The New Guy steeled himself and turned to the tree.

There was no blood, no shattered furry corpse.

He walked closer, closer. He found a neat hole in the tree, where he had last seen the monkey's head. He looked behind the slender trunk: a crater of splintered tree-flesh and shredded bark.

He stared.

The sergeant staggered to his feet and whacked dust from his pants. "The––*hic*–monkey *moved,* you fuckhead," he crowed. "You shot the fucking rope."

* * *

Keeler sat, submissive, spooked, on the floor in front of a coffee table while the little man from Philco Ford silently scraped vegetables onto her plate.

The room was twice as large as her own, and was furnished in Spartan style: a neatly-made bed, a tiny couch, a desk and chair. High shelves lined with books, their titles muffled by candlelight. The Formica table and, on it, a double-burner hotplate, two stoneware dishes, and chopsticks engraved with gold letters.

The man lowered himself to the floor across from her.

"If I'm going to eat with you," she said, "I should at least know your name."

He picked up his chopsticks. Without the baseball cap, he looked young. Her own age, perhaps.

"My name," she said loudly, "is–"

"I know perfectly well who you are, Lieutenant Keeler." His

English was unaccented. "Pleased to meet you. I'm John Kim. By the way," he added, "I like your hair. New style, right?"

Keeler dropped her chopsticks.

John Kim smiled. "Sorry I didn't answer your questions—you know, before—but I knew I wouldn't be able to keep a straight face."

"You...you're—-American?"

"Korean. But I got my engineering degree at UCLA."

She stared at him, open-mouthed.

"Eat, Lieutenant. Before it gets cold. I make a mean stir-fry, but it gets greasy if you leave it sitting around." His eyes twinkled. "You do know how to use chopsticks? Or should I beg a fork from the German guy next door?"

She picked up her chopsticks. "God," she said. "I feel like a real ass. *UCLA.* And here I am, sounding like Tonto."

He chuckled.

She sighed. "White woman heap big shithead, Kemo Sabe."

"To be fair, I encouraged it. I'm sorry."

She eyed him severely. "No, you're not."

He deftly lifted a bite of vegetable and rice between his sticks. "You're right. I was having a great time. Eat." He put the food in his mouth.

She nibbled a carrot strip. "Hey, this is good. I mean, really good. Spicy. Wow."

"I'm glad you like it. My college roommate always told me, 'A man has to have a culinary specialty to impress chicks.' He was a pasta man, spaghetti a la vodka. Me, I have stir-fry. Makes me seem more exotic. More—"

"Korean," she said. "This is seriously great." She picked up a green bean. "You get all your dates this way?"

"You mean, by carting away boxed monkeys for them?"

She dropped the bean. "Shit! You *did* know?"

He rolled his eyes.

"Then—what did—where did—-"

"I followed your orders. I took it to the USO club at the beach."

"You opened the box."

His smile dimpled his left cheek. "Nope. Didn't even peek through the holes."

"Right. Then how did you know what was inside?"

"Simple. I know books. I have a few myself. And I know monkeys. Particularly the Major's monkey, whose busy little fingers have done more to keep me and my boys in business than sabotage or even this country's primitive electrical service. There's a basic difference between monkeys and books, even taped up in boxes." He favored her once more with his left dimple. "Books," he said, "do not fart."

* * *

The Medic heard it first: a mewling, not unlike the cry of a baby. He pulled his buddy to a halt. "Listen."

His buddy listened. "It could be a trap."

"What kind of trap would sound like that?"

"Leave it alone."

"Leave it *alone*? Are you nuts?"

"What if it's a *baby*?" said the buddy. "You know. Gooks leave a baby in the jungle, booby-trap it, we pick it up–"

Comrades slogged past them. "Maynard, get your ass in gear," said one.

"Move it or lose it," said another.

Mewl. Leaves twitched, fell still. The Medic pointed. "Right there. I'm going to check it out."

"Shit, Maynard, don't. What if it's a booby-trap?"

The Medic shrugged off his pack and set it on the dirt track. He picked up his weapon, took a cautious step into the grass. Another step. He parted the leaves with his M-16's barrel.

"Jesus," he said.

"It better not be a fucking baby," his buddy called. "Whatever it is, don't fuckin' touch it—"

"It's a monkey. Looks like he's stuck; there's something around his neck, looks like." The Medic stepped carefully toward the bushes. Two men stopped next to the buddy to watch.

"What's that?" said one.

"A monkey," said the buddy.

"Shit," said the second. "Let's get out of here, man—sucker's probably booby-trapped."

The Medic slung his M-16 over his shoulder. "He's not booby-trapped. He's moving—he'd've blown up by now." He drew his knife and cut the tangled rope from the animal's neck. He lifted the monkey gently. It weighed practically nothing. It stared at him with ancient, solemn eyes.

The buddy assessed the monkey in the Medic's arms. "Look at that face. Looks like he's a hundred years old."

"Poor little guy." One of the men with the buddy touched the monkey's face, jerked his hand back. "*Fuck! Sonovabitch!*" Blood trickled down his finger.

Cradled in the Medic's arms, the monkey bared his teeth.

"Must be hungry," mused the Medic's buddy. He pulled a tropical Hershey's bar from his pocket, stripped off its wrapper, handed it, gingerly, to the monkey. "Here you go, guy."

The monkey took it, sniffed it, and tossed it over his shoulder.

* * *

"Are you okay?"

Keeler squinted up from beneath her Smokey-the-Bear hat; she focused red-rimmed eyes on John Kim's face. "Yeah." The cigarette bobbed in her mouth.

"Is there something I could do to help?"

"No." Keeler fished another cigarette from her pack, lit it off

129

the first. "Sorry. No."

"Then I'll come back to claim you when you finish." He tipped back her hat and kissed her on the forehead.

Keeler watched him walk away. *You're too good, too sweet*, she thought as she smoked. *I don't deserve anybody's love.* She saw again, again, the hairy face matted with pizza sauce.

The monkey is dead. I have killed the monkey.

She heard again, again, the Major's muffled sobs.

There, there...

She sucked in smoke, pulled the hat from her head, raked her fingers through short, sweat-limp auburn curls. A tear dribbled down her chin. *Only God can help me.*

She had to do it. Though it would humiliate her. Though it would certainly lead to the Major. To condemnation.

Perhaps to prison.

I have no choice. Only God. The monkey is dead.

I have killed the monkey.

* * *

The Supply Sergeant chomped the butt of an evil-looking stogie. "Now what would I want a monkey for?"

The Medic scratched his head. It itched something terrible these days. "You could keep him for a pet. Or maybe trade him for something."

The Supply Sergeant—huge, well-muscled, profoundly black—squatted down to look at the monkey. The monkey looked back. He was licking a lollipop.

"We found him on the way back. Been dragging him around with us two days now. It's a damned good thing we didn't run into Charlie; dunno what I'd of done with the little guy." The Medic hung his head. "Some of the guys...well, you know the guys, some of them. They'd just as soon leash him up, make him walk point. Frankly, Sarge,

130

I'm kinda scared for him."

The Supply Sergeant stood up, removed his stogie, and spat on the dry dead earth.

"Clancy named him 'John Wayne,'" offered the Medic.

The monkey blinked twice and stuck out his tongue, tinted deep green from the candy.

"What's he eat?" asked the Supply Sergeant.

"Just about everything we eat. Likes tinned meat, biscuits, those little cakes from the kits. Candy. He don't like jungle Hersheys, though."

Can't fault him for that, thought the Supply Sergeant. He reached a meaty hand down toward the monkey.

"Go easy, Sarge. If he gets spooked, he, ah, nips."

The Supply Sergeant drew back his hand. He reached into his trouser pocket and pulled out a piece of salt water taffy.

The monkey watched the huge hand open, to reveal a pink, half-squashed nugget. He dropped the lollipop stick and picked up the taffy daintily, with two fingers.

The Supply Sergeant spoke around his cigar. "You got good taste, Duke."

The monkey grinned, stretching his lip.

The Supply Sergeant reached down again, showed the monkey a pink, empty palm. "I'm afraid that's all I can spare," he said.

The monkey grabbed the empty hand, turned it over, and bit it soundly.

The cigar butt hit the dirt.

* * *

"Bless me, Father, for I have sinned..."

Keeler touched her forehead to the curtain separating her from Father LeMieux. He knew who she was: *she* had approached *him*, after all. But he had insisted that she use this makeshift confessional.

Tradition, he'd said. Reassurance.

She had to admit, it was reassuring. She tried the Sign of the Cross, and got it right. *Like riding a bicycle.* "My last worthy confession was...uh...three years ago?"

"That's quite all right," said Father LeMieux through the curtain. "God treasures his prodigals. Please, continue."

"Since then, I've...uh...fornicated...oh, I don't know how many times–"

"Numbers are not really important, my dear."

"Uh. Okay. Well, I've..." She began to sweat. "I've taken the lord's name in vain, oh, lots. Practically all the time, I'm afraid." The curtain brushed her bangs, electrifying them. She licked her lips. "I've lied. I've cheated at poker. I yelled at the Mama-san who does the laundry for no really good reason and killed the Major's monkey, and I've lied–"

"You've said that already," said the priest. "That you lied."

Silence. She held her breath.

"Now. About the Major's monkey."

Keeler's stomach knotted; perspiration dripped from the short hairs at the nape of her neck. She touched her breast pocket, felt the reassuring crinkle of a pack of Winstons.

An eternity passed.

"Are you truly sorry about...everything?"

"Oh, yes, Father. You know I am."

"Even about the Major's monkey?"

"Oh, God. Especially that. It's–it's driving me nuts."

Silence. Then, "It's not easy–"

She listened attentively.

He cleared his throat. "It's not–" Ahem. "You must put aside the animosity you felt toward the Major's–"

His voice had grown husky, risen, become unsteady.

"Father? Are you okay?"

"Yes, my dear. Ah." He inhaled noisily. "You really...did you really kill the Major's monkey?"

She hung her head. "I had him killed. I tranquilized him and sent him off to a homicidal friend of mine. And now he's dead." She paused. "The monkey's dead. Not my friend." She nibbled her fingernail, listening, ear to the curtain.

A soft, rhythmic, almost inaudible sobbing.

No. Father LeMieux was...*laughing*.

Keeler pulled out the cigarette pack, pressed it between her hands. "Father. You've got to help me out here."

"Oh—-ah—-Hee. I'm, ah, sorry about this, my dear. Please... forgive me. Please. But...ah, I'm afraid that monkey was...not one of my favorites." Father LeMieux blew his nose lustily. "Conlon left the sacristy open one day, and he devoured the entire supply of sacred hosts." His voice became solemn. "It wasn't his fault, really. We should've locked them up."

"Jesus."

Father LeMieux sighed. "So, my dear, I, too, have harbored... unkind thoughts toward the Major's monkey. You know," he added quietly, "There's a rumor circulating that you had something to do with his disappearance."

"Oh, shit." She fingered out a cigarette, slipped the pack back into her pocket.

"Now, now. Just a rumor. You have been vocal in your criticism of the...unfortunate creature, you know. And everyone knew about your hair." He lowered his voice to a near-whisper. "Don't worry. I will never confirm that rumor. Confidentiality of the confessional."

"Thank God."

"You're welcome." *Ahem.* "I would apprise you that this confidentiality goes two ways, Lieutenant."

"Beg pardon?"

"I would ask you not to divulge what I told you about my opinion of the, ah, deceased."

"Of course not."

"I should not have burdened you with that information. May God forgive me."

"Sure, Father."

"But of course, my own weaknesses—" He cleared his throat, then said, quite delicately, "Well, that doesn't absolve you of your sin, now, does it."

"No. Of course not."

He paused. "You're sure he's dead. The monkey."

"I'm sure."

"Oh."

She thought she heard a giggle. "Father?"

"Yes, my dear?"

"My penance?"

"Oh. I'm terribly sorry. I guess I got off the track. Forgive me."

"It's okay."

"For your penance." He inhaled slowly. "Say five 'Hail Marys' and five 'Our Fathers.'"

"That's it?" Keeler stared at the curtain. "That's all I get for three years of sin and killing the Major's monkey?"

"You could say a rosary, too, if it makes you feel better."

"Don't I have to make reparation? Don't I have to confess to the Major and offer, I don't know...to buy her a new monkey or something?" Keeler felt nauseated. *Where was the absolution in five "Hail Marys" and five "Our Fathers?"*

"If you had killed the Major, I would have to advise you to turn yourself in to the MPs," said the priest evenly. "However, the Major believes her monkey is alive. This is, in fact, the Major's fervent hope. It would be cruel to dash the Major's fervent hope, don't you think?"

"I–I don't know."

"Well, then. How about, you resolve from this time forth to be doubly kind to animals, as a sign to God of your Firm Purpose of Amendment?"

She sat numbly while Father LeMieux pronounced his

absolution. If he absolved her, God absolved her, didn't he?

Didn't he?

She glanced at her cigarette.

It was crushed flat and bent in three places.

* * *

"You say this monkey's worth five poncho liners." The Captain leaned back in his chair. Behind him was a small window; through it, the Supply Sergeant could see the misty green hills of Pleiku.

"Yep," said the Supply Sergeant. He kept his poker face.

The Captain folded his hands on his desk. "With the rainy season coming on, it would be nice to have a morale booster of some sort. I think Col. Harkins would welcome your little fellow at the 71st. 'John Wayne,' eh?"

The Supply Sergeant nodded solemnly. Heh, heh: Yes, he had himself a sense of humor, and it was dark as his face. He also had himself an excellent memory: if this officious little motherfucker hadn't screwed him two months ago, hadn't shorted him on numbers in several cartons, the Supply Sergeant would still be eating freeze-dried corned-beef hash.

The Captain smiled. "Good name. Col. Harkins is a big fan of The Duke."

The Supply Sergeant *loved* freeze-dried corned-beef hash. Loved it like a fine cigar. But only Airborne got freeze-dried rations. And they kept their supplies close.

So close, he didn't know how this skinny-assed Captain got to them. Make no mistake: the Supply Sergeant was building his own lines. But that was beside the point. The point was, *Fuck with Sarge, and there will be consequences.*

"You're coming up Tuesday for a run?" The Captain twiddled a pencil in his long, white, privileged fingers. "Why don't you bring him with you."

135

The Supply Sergeant rose, saluted solidly. "And my poncho liners?"

"Uh-uh-uh: payment upon delivery. You know my policy." The Captain returned the salute, smartly, from his seat. "By the bye, Sarge, what happened to your hand?"

The Supply Sergeant kept his poker face. "Hand?"

"Your right hand. I noticed when you saluted—"

The Supply Sergeant dipped his bandaged hand in his breast pocket and drew out an evil-looking cigar. "Cut it on a metal rack in the depot." He pulled the cellophane from the stogie and turned to go.

"Oh. Almost forgot—what does John Wayne eat?"

The Supply Sergeant turned back. "Whatever you put in front of him." He gave the Captain a slow smile.

The Captain nodded. "Good. Good."

"I'm sure he'll be a hit in Pleiku," said the Supply Sergeant. He stuck the cigar between his teeth. "He'll add a certain *something* to the atmosphere."

* * *

PFC Garabedian plopped a scoop of barbecue onto Keeler's bun. "There you go, Lieutenant." He winked. "*Mystery* meat."

She halted. "What is that supposed to mean?"

The private smiled. "You know. Mystery meat."

She stared at him. "I resent the implication."

"Implication?" The private looked confused. "I was just...you know. Hell, Lieutenant. *Mystery* meat." He shrugged. "It's a joke, is all," said Garabedian.

Keeler swallowed. "Sorry." She picked up her tray, her hands trembling. "Long day at the war."

She sat down at the long table, followed by Zytch and Reno. She lit a cigarette, took a puff, examined the heap of steaming meat.

There was a hair. In the barbecue. Short, brown.

Monkey-colored.

She dropped the cigarette, leapt up, ran outside.

As she retched behind the building, a hand touched her shoulder. She jumped.

"Keeler?" Zytch's round face puckered with concern. "Geez. You look like shit."

Keeler steadied a hand against the wall.

Two young men in OR scrubs passed. One elbowed the other, pointed to the puddle of vomit. "Y'know, Montgomery," he said, "tonight's special don't look so special."

Keeler mopped her forehead with her sleeve. " I think—"

"You think what?" Zytch handed her a kleenix.

Keeler wiped her mouth. "I'll be all right. Really. It's just...I don't think I'm going to eat meat again."

"You've developed a craving for boiled potatoes and canned peas?"

Keeler shuddered. "It's just—" She swallowed a belch.

"Yeah?"

"Meat. You never know what's in it."

* * *

The Major was singing "Bali Hai"; she had just reached the last "Come a-away," when the hand reached into her stall and stole her shampoo. She gasped.

"*Sage?*"

It couldn't be. She was in a shower in Pleiku, where she had come to visit her old friend Colonel Bernard.

Surely, it couldn't be.

"Sage," she said softly, hopefully.

She heard only the sputter of the shower. She looked down. Yes. The shampoo was indeed gone.

She dressed quickly, still wet, in her clean fatigues. Her heart trip-hammered as she crossed the compound. Quickly, because black clouds had gathered and she knew better than to dally. Quickly, because—

Don't be an idiot, she told herself firmly. *Just because you want it, doesn't make it real.*

The rain rattled down as she stomped into the Female Officers' hooch. "Bernie?" she called.

Colonel Bernard popped out of her room, a bottle of whiskey in her hand. "Why, there you are. Let's have us a little something while we wait for the rain to let up."

"Bernie—there isn't a *monkey* on this compound, is there?" The Major held her breath.

"Why, yes. There is." Colonel Bernard pulled her into her room and set out two glasses. "I'm afraid we're out of ice," she said. "The machine at the club seems to be broken."

The Major's head reeled. "This monkey—"

"Oh, he's a pistol." Bernie poured the whiskey. "He belongs to the registrar. Someone brought him in from the jungle—"

"He's wild?" The Major's heart stopped.

"Oh, dear...I don't think so. What I meant to say is, he was at some jungle outpost, they say. Anyway, I *hate* the thing." She took a sip. "I love cats, you know, but I never much cared for monkeys. And this one is just *awful.* He chews on electrical wires, and he steals everything that isn't nailed down. Acts just like he owns the place. And he has a problem with—" she lowered her voice—"gas. Probably all that candy; he stole Marge Reginald's entire stash of candy from home. I think it was Hershey's kisses, or maybe those little bars you pass out at Halloween—"

The Major gulped her whiskey and walked out.

"Wait, where are you going? It's raining cats and—"

The Major marched out into the rainy, muddy hospital yard.

She threw the door to the company office open with a bang. She bowled past clerks, through partitions, into the back office, trailing confusion and black combat-boot tracks.

Major George S. Timmory looked up from the current issue of *Stars and Stripes* to see a big-boned, square-shouldered woman whose soggy fatigues were plastered to her body. Her hair was a fright of dripping red curls, her face a clenched fist. She leaned over him, dripping rain on the newspaper in fat blobbed drops.

"Where's Sage?" she demanded.

Major George S. Timmory rose. "What's a sage?" His voice squeaked.

"My *monkey*!" She thundered. "*Sage*. Where is he, you *runt*?"

"Oh. The monkey." He blinked. "He's yours?"

"Give me my monkey, you little faggot, or I'll cram that newspaper down your throat."

Major George S. Timmory stepped back. "Oh," he said. "Ah. The monkey. John Wayne?"

"*Sage*!" she roared.

"Ah. Sage." Clerks peeped around the partitions. He shrugged. "If he's yours, well then, you just take him."

The Major stood up straight and looked down upon him. "Take him?"

"Why, yes. I don't know where he is right now, but you can certainly have him. I've only had him a couple of days, myself. Won him in a poker game." He scratched his head. "The funny thing is, I don't usually win. But he's yours if you want him."

She looked aggrieved. "You don't want my little wise man."

Major George S. Timmory cleared his throat. "Well, it's not that I don't *like* him...I mean, he's all right. As monkeys go. But if he's yours, well, I don't think it's wise to squabble about it. You can have him. Please. I don't know where he is right now---he's never really where you expect him to be---but I'm sure he'll be back. Then, well, just take him."

A smile slowly worked its way to her lips, and he noted that it made her...well, *attractive*. He hastily pulled his chair to the side of the

139

desk. "Just have a seat here, Major. John Wayne will be right back, I'm sure."

"Sage," she said.

"Sage," he said. "Sage. Um. Would you like something while you wait? Coffee?" He lowered his voice. "I have a Snickers bar."

She smiled fully, radiantly. "Certainly, Major. A Snickers would be wonderful."

He opened his desk drawer, peeked in, rifled about. "Oh, dear." Major George S. Timmory blushed to the roots of his sparse, sandy hair. "That's funny. They were here before lunch. But—" he looked up at her—"they seem to be *gone*."

* * *

Spec 4 Gonzo Carter cringed as Doc Hoerner slowly injected novocain into the flesh of his palm. "Attaboy," said the doctor.

The Lieutenant peered at the wound and whistled. "You could get a purple heart for this. You try to feed him?" she said, swabbing his hand with betadine.

Carter closed his eyes. "Tried *not* to feed him," he said through clenched teeth. Tried not to feed the little fucker his Good & Plentys; tried to pry them loose. Damn!

The little fucker was going to die.

Doc Hoerner clipped the needle into a holder. "I thought Keeler had managed to kill the beast."

Carter'd heard rumors, too. That was back when the little fucker used to hang out in her hooch. Back when she'd had stuff in her hooch worth its time. But there wasn't nothing good in Keeler's hooch now. No candy, no pizza—just fruit and vegetables; Keeler was on some bizarre *Buddhist* kick, probably something she picked up from that new boyfriend of hers. What was he? Japanese, Chinese, Korean? She'd even given up smoking. Again.

"Feel that?" said Doc Hoerner.

"No." He'd felt a little sorry for the critter back then, when he'd heard those rumors. But now, the little fucker's *back*. Like a cat that won't drown.

The doctor stitched. "Now, sponge," he said. "He raided my hooch once. Chewed up my cigars. That's when I got my padlock. Had the Philco Ford guys install the bracket, and it's been worth its weight in gold. What about you?" He flicked a glance over his mask at the Lieutenant. "He ever hit you?"

"Nah. He knows I respect him. I mean, what the hell, he was here first." She sponged the wound. "He had primate-cy, so to speak."

"Groan," said the doctor.

Carter glanced at his palm; it had stopped bleeding, but it was some *ugly*.

This wasn't funny.

With the Major gone to Pleiku every time she had a day off, the little fucker was running around like a kid without a momma. Twice this week, it'd trashed the OR hooch. Not the entire hooch, mind you; just his very own personal quarters—wide open, nothing he could put a padlock on. He watched with fascinated horror as Doc Hoerner dug in the needle. Well, one of these days—soon—the Major was going come back from her little Festival of Love and find her sorry-assed little buddy AWOL. Permanently.

The squinty-eyed bastard had met his match.

With his free hand, Carter dug savagely at his neatly-trimmed afro. The Lieutenant dabbed his wound; the doctor tied another knot.

Fuck, yeah: the Major's monkey had to die.

And he, Spec 4 Gonzo Carter, was going to see to it personally.

And this time, the little motherfucker was gonna *stay* dead.

Waiting for Charlie

In the little staff lounge outside the operating rooms at the 27th Surgical Hospital in Chu Lai, Viet Nam, surgical nurse Captain Posy Felton and her rag-tag crew of O.R. technicians fought to hold the Enemy—the tedium of a day with no patients—at bay with the most meager of weapons.

For PFC Deke J. Montgomery III, it was a small volume on the Psychology of Golf. For Spec. 4 Gonzo Carter, a slender paperback with the author's haughty black face on the cover. In the rear echelon— the battered easy chair in the far corner of the lounge—Pvt. Harold "Lucky" Lukan wielded a well-thumbed leather-bound tome.

The Captain herself brandished the latest issue of *Stars and Stripes*.

Alas, it was a losing battle. "Damn, I'm bored," said Captain Felton.

Carter raised his eyes to the window. "Was that a chopper?"

"I certainly hope not," said Montgomery from behind his book. "I need to sit. My feet are killing me."

Carter snorted. "We been sitting on our butts all day." He closed his book and sighed. "I can't stand this shit. I'm gonna kill myself." He pulled a pack of cigarettes from his pocket and shook one out. "Fuck, where's Charlie when we need him?"

"You can't smoke that in here," said Mongomery. "Oxygen tanks. Captain, he's going to smoke that in here."

The Captain reached out; Carter shook a second cigarette from his pack and laid it on her palm.

In the corner, his big frame curled in the chair, Lucky Lukan read.

"What's on the radio?" asked the captain.

Carter thought. "'Easy Listening in the Late Afternoon.'"

"Better'n nothing," said the Captain.

"Yeah? Well, not much." Carter flipped the switch on the radio that sat on the chipped Formica top of the coffee table. He thumbed the dial: strains of "Moon River" oozed from the speaker. Carter's black face went sour. "Don't come much whiter than that," he said. "Except that little fucker Pat Boone."

The Captain lit her cigarette.

"And what's wrong with Pat Boone?" Montgomery asked.

Carter glared at him and shook his head.

The Captain turned a page.

"Oh, wow," said Montgomery, his eyes on his book.

"Something exciting you'd like to share?" said the Captain.

Montgomery raised an eyebrow over his wire-rimmed glasses. "It's a great tip on how to avoid slicing the ball."

"Oh." The Captain stretched. "That would be exciting, if I played golf."

"You should, you know. It's tremendous exercise, the walking, the swing—"

Carter snorted.

Montgomery ignored him and peered over his glasses at the Captain. "Beautiful countryside. Always. My father—" His Massachusetts accent morphed the word into *fathah*—"has a membership at the Hyannis club, on the Cape. A bit too windy for my taste, but the ocean view? Stupendous."

Carter smiled toothily. "Sounds like my kind of place."

Montgomery paid him no mind. "I've played with the Kennedys there, as a kid," he told the Captain, who had returned to her newspaper. "The cousins."

"So." Carter blew smoke at Montgomery. "You gonna invite me to this Hyena's club, we get back to the world?"

Montgomery flicked him a look and returned to his reading. Tony Bennett crooned about misplacing his heart.

The Captain turned a page.

Montgomery yawned, patting his open mouth daintily.

Carter frowned into his book.

In the corner, Lucky Lukan's blond eyebrows knit as he read.

The Captain glanced out the window. "God, I'm bored," she said. "This is worse than playing golf."

Carter snickered, and Montgomery pushed his glasses up on his nose with an injured air. "You're only saying that because you haven't tried it," he said. "You know, Captain, you have a sweet little course right in your back yard."

The Captain flicked her ash. "You mean up by the tire factory? The place with the clown and the giant windmill?"

"I mean French Lick," said Montgomery.

The Captain smiled. "Ah. French Lick. Much as I do love that name, I believe that's in Indiana. I'm from Cleveland. Cleveland's in Ohio."

"Indiana, Ohio." Montgomery waved his hand.

Carter rolled his eyes and crushed his cigarette butt against the top of the coffee table.

The Captain turned a page in her paper. "Gonzo, looks like your Cubs are first place in the East."

"Fuck yeah," said Carter. "Think they'd send me home to cheer 'em on?"

"Might as well, for all the good we're doing here. Ah, lord. The Indians are plain useless." The Captain glanced at Carter's book. "What's that you're reading?" He held it up for her. "LeRoi Jones. Who's that?"

"Poet."

"You're reading poetry?"

Montgomery pointed limp-wristedly at Carter. Lisped, "'I think that I will never see/ a poem as lov-ah-lee as *he*–'"

Carter turned back two pages and read fiercely, a passage about raping white girls and their fathers and cutting the mothers' throats.

He glared at Montgomery.

The Captain nodded. "LeRoi Jones. I'll have to remember

that, next time I need some light reading."

"He's changed his name," said Carter. "He's Amiri Baraka now, if you want to find his stuff."

"Oh? He's Muslim?" said the Captain. "Like Cassius Clay, Muhammed Ali?"

Montgomery pushed his glasses up on his nose. "Muhammed Ali. Hah!"

Carter closed his book. "And just what about Muhammed Ali makes you Hah?"

"That was just a publicity stunt, changing his name. He'd do ANYthing for the spotlight. Like flunking the Service exam."

"Muhammed Ali," Carter's voice was menacing, "failed that examination on purpose. He didn't believe Black men should go out and kill Yellow men for the White man. That took courage, man."

Montgomery stuck out his underdeveloped chin. "Coming *here*," he said, "that's what takes courage."

"Not for me, man. It just took a honky draft board."

"I volunteered," said Montgomery. "My *fathah* tried to talk me out of it, but I *wanted* to serve my country." He sniffed. "Flunking a test is a coward's way out."

"I bet you'd feel that way if you were out humping the jungle," said Carter.

"It wouldn't make a bit of difference."

"Right," said Carter. "Yessir, I would pay to see that."

The Captain crushed her cigarette against the Formica. "Boys, boys, boys."

Carter threw Montgomery a toxic look.

The Captain rattled her newspaper.

In the corner, Lucky Lukan's eyes followed his big finger across the page.

Montgomery licked his thumb savagely and turned a page.

The Captain skimmed the funnies. "Steve Roper, Terry and the Pirates, Rex Morgan." She sighed. "God. Only thing worth reading is Peanuts."

Carter lumbered out of his chair and stretched his back. "Damn. Where's Charlie? He give up?" He squinted out the window at the sun-bleached, empty helipad, then sat back down. "Hey, Captain, gimme some of that paper."

The Captain peeled off the first four pages of the Stars and Stripes and handed them to him.

Carter lit up another cigarette. "I'm gonna kill myself," he said.

"You shouldn't smoke in here," said Montgomery.

The Captain put out her hand. Carter laid a cigarette on her palm.

"Hey!" Carter turned up the radio. "It's 'The Young Sound.'"

R-E-S-P-E-C-T, sang Aretha Franklin. Carter held his cigarette in the air and bopped in his seat to the rhythm.

Aretha yielded to Simon and Garfunkel. Carter sucked in smoke and bent over the newspaper.

The Captain hummed along with *Scarborough Fair* and turned a page.

Montgomery drew a pen from his scrub shirt pocket and underlined a passage in his book.

In the corner, Lucky Lukan read, his lips forming silent words.

Carter looked up. "Hey, Montgomery. Your Daddy plays golf with the Kennedys, right?"

Montgomery made another mark. "Yes, *Cahtah*. What of it?"

Carter grinned and tapped the paper. "Another story today about Teddy K, that little fucker that swims so good. Catch this, it's right up your alley." He read aloud about how the judge in the Chappaquidic case had settled on Martha's Vineyard because of its long golf season. "Guess we know where to find justice in America, don't we?"

Montgomery turned a page.

Carter said, "Article goes on to say how the judge's got to take time out from his game to run that inquest for the girl that drowned in Teddy's car." Tsk, tsk. "You been following this situation, Montgomery?"

Montgomery made a note in the margin of his page.

"Says here, the judge thinks Teddy's been punished enough." Tsk, tsk. "So he gives him an itsy-bitsy jail sentence. Then, why, he *suspends* it." Carter folded his hands piously. "Oh, Lord, turn me white, so I can get away with murder."

Montgomery stared fixedly at his page. His ears grew red.

"Now, what if?" said Carter. "What if, say, Teddy was a Brother? Not a Kennedy brother, but a *Brother*? You think that judge would take time off from his golf game to keep his black ass out of jail?"

The Captain blew a smoke ring. "Boys, boys, boys."

Montgomery stuck out his lower lip. "I hardly think—"

The balding head of Doc Hoerner poked through the doorframe. The Captain, Carter and Montgomery looked up. In the corner, a fly zigged a drunken circle around Lucky Lukan's bent head, docked on his mountainous shoulder. He read, sweat beading his pale, furrowed brow.

"Hey, Dan," said the Captain. "S'up?"

Yo, doc!" Carter saluted the surgeon pompously. "We are at the ready here. We are pumped to hump. Just give us the word."

"You got something for us?" Montgomery asked.

Hoerner smiled. "Great news. I just checked the office. They say nothing's coming. So enjoy yourselves. I just wanted you guys to know I'm in the mess hall if you need me."

He turned and walked away, whistling *Guantanamera*.

"Shit," said Carter. He turned a page. "Charlie, where the fuck are you? Don't anybody get shot anymore?"

Montgomery pushed up his glasses and resumed reading, pen poised above his book.

The Captain sized up the day's pin-up photo: all legs and boobs and teeth, plus a cowboy hat. She shook her head and turned the page.

In the corner, Lucky Lukan unwound himself from his easy

chair. He stood up, a mountain of a man, the great leather-bound book clamped in his hand. He fixed them with feverish eyes.

"You poor fools," he said.

Montgomery glanced up, pen hovering. "I beg your pardon?"

Carter lowered his paper. "Luck?"

"Lukan?" said the Captain.

Lucky Lukan's voice was low, urgent. "It's all here, in Alma 5-37, and you just can't see it." He opened the black-bound volume, balanced it on the flat of a thick palm, read slowly, ominously, "O ye workers of iniquity; ye that are puffed up in the vain things of the world—" His voice gathered power: "Ye that have professed to have known the ways of righteousness nevertheless have gone astray, as sheep having no shepherd," he thumped the page with a finger the size of a cigar, "Notwithstanding a shepherd hath called after you *and is still calling after you—*"

Carter stared, fingering his chin.

Montgomery's eyebrows inched into his hairline; his glasses slid down his nose unchallenged.

The Captain frowned. "This is some kind of joke, right?"

Lucky Lukan gave each, in turn, a look of great pity. "'And now,'" he read, "'if ye are not the sheep of the good shepherd, of what fold are ye?'" His voice trembled. "'Behold, I say unto you, that the devil is your shepherd.'" He thumped the book. "The devil." *Thump.* "The *devil!*" His voice caught. "I accepted this as my mission. I thought I could show you the way—" His eyes shone, and he flipped the pages in his book half-heartedly. "Even *that's* in here—" He cited a chapter and verse, and began, from memory, "'*I say unto you—*'" Suddenly, his face went blank; his eyes dulled. And Lucky Lukan stumbled from the room.

The Byrds sang *Hey, Mister Tambourine Man.*

Nobody spoke.

At last, the Captain said, "Jesus H. Christ."

Montgomery looked confused. "Where's Alma in the Bible? Is

that the one after Kings?"

Carter gave him a look. "There ain't no Alma. That ain't no *Bible*. I saw it." He nodded slowly. "Big white motherfucker, keeps to himself, wouldn't say 'shit' if he had a mouth full. Sure."

"Sure?" said the Captain.

"Sure. It's the Book of Mormon." Carter bared his teeth in a grin. "Luck's a *Mormon Missionary*."

"Wow." The Captain squashed out her cigarette. "No shit."

"No shit. Explains all them white shirts in his footlocker." Carter picked up his section of the paper.

"Think you know a guy," mused the Captain.

"Luck?" Carter shrugged. "Ain't nobody really knows that mother."

Montgomery held up his book on the Psychology of Golf. "You know Billy Casper's a Mormon? It says so right here. How's that for coincidence!"

Carter rolled his eyes and sighed. "I'm gonna kill myself." He shook two cigarettes out of his pack and handed one to the Captain. "Damn. Where the hell's Charlie?"

"Carter," Montgomery whined, "you *know* you can't smoke in here."

Medcap

So we go out in the jeeps an a deuce-and-a-half, cause you gotta have something big for all of us an the tables an the chair—portable dentist chair, see, folds up but its still one heavy fucker. And we maybe got a shitload of docs nurses medics interpreters an one dentist, whoevers around that day. We take lots of aspirin no sweat pills penicillin quinine, that shorta shit. Lots of wintergreen oil, gooks love wintergreen oil, dont ask me why. Cant drink the shit—smells like ya can but the stuffll kill ya. Dont know what the fuck they use it for but they *ask* for it, man. Like its got a reputation or somethin.

We go out an hole up in this wood shack, like an old store or somethin, an we call em, let em know we come. Most days the gooks they line up, man. An the docs ask em what they need, give em pills shots stuff for TB, lots of ems got TB. Shit, *most* of ems got TB. Always lotsa little kids hangin out, pullin the hair on our arms an laughin an stuff, cute little fuckers, we bring em candy. The docs an nurses they try ta give the kids shots for cholera an typhoid an stuff, an we go around with the interpreters an tell em its good for em an safe. No shit, man, you try tellin some gook mamasan yer gonna make their kid safe from cholera by stickin a needle in their arm. I mean I dont speak Vietnamese cept a few words like *dinky-dow* an *deety-mau*, an they dont speak English cept maybe *numba one* an *numba ten*, see, so we gotta use the interpreters, but still, howya sposed to tell some mamasan we aint gonna kill her little kid stickin this bigassed fuckin needle in that little skinny arm, even if you got the words in Vietnamese. The kids in good shape, aint got cholera to begin with, howya gonna tell em he wont get it if he gets this shot, when they dont know what cholera fuckin is, even. Honest ta god, its a fuckin miracle they go for it. Lots of times they dont. Whatya gonna do, man.

Most days we see some weird shit, like these big old sores, man—sometimes so bad theyre runnin pus. Or they got an arm big as a circus fatlady or their toes is black or theres a bone got broke an just stayed that way. Had one kid got a lump size of a fuckin football on his head an a temp of 104. One time, man, was this mamasan had this thing on her neck thats, like, out to *here*. Make ya wanna fuckin puke I swear ta god.

One thing them gooks really go for more n even the wintergreen oil, thats that chair, man. They line up a mile for that chair. Dentist always does a helluva business, puts em in the chair an pulls out teeth. Right an left. Dont fill no cavities, just pulls them teeth right out, man. We sittin around, hes workin his ass off sweatin like a sonovabitch yankin out teeth right an left. Days real busy he lines em up an numbs em all first, works on em once the novocaine takes hold one after another, pullin out teeth. The gooks dont care if they got this big old gap in their teeth I guess, just sos it dont hurt no more.

I spose we might save some kids with the penicillin or maybe even the cholera shots. *If* they take em. Maybe we cure some a the whores so they dont give us back the drip or the syph. Maybe we make some old mamasans TB better or maybe the quinine fixes somebodys malaria.

But for my money when it comes ta winnin hearts an minds, man, I say hands down no shit absolute *numba one* no contest, its gotta be that fuckin dentist chair.

Three Minor Love Stories

David's eyes were huge and brown and deep as the abyss and there were secrets hidden in them. When he nodded off after lazy night love in Mattie's narrow bed, secrets leaked through the cracks of his sleep and escaped in small, potent cries.

He was not her first, but he taught her many things. Techniques; touches. Not to fear the mystery of his large, strange and distinctly other body. These things he gave her, but he kept the secrets to himself, and Mattie did not ask. His were the secrets of an infantry lieutenant in the Americal Division. The times when he came close to giving voice to even the smallest of them—when he'd had too much to drink (often, now that he had returned from the jungles for good), or when he bit her neck hard or locked her in an embrace that squeezed her ribs and lungs, or when she gasped beneath the leaden weight of him—those times, she realized that she lacked the strength to succor his ghosts.

He was the kind of man who talked casually of small things, ate heartily, laughed easily and would leave no note when he committed suicide.

But one who is locked in an asylum might well cling to another whose insanity is less abrasive than his companions'. One who is drowning in a swamp might well fight through barbed wire to attain a treacherous and puddle-ridden high ground. Mattie was crazy about him, loved him in the skewed way that a woman can love a man she could never know in a world lurid with blood and lies.

The night before David was to go home, they made love to each other softly, tenderly, absently. Then he left. No expectations; no promises; no letters.

Life went on in Viet Nam, with its blood, maiming and death, and its hellos and goodbyes.

Two months later, Mattie shared her bed with a nurse anesthetist, a good man with no secrets except Mattie, kept in careful kindness from his wife back home. When he left, toward the end of her own time in-country, she took shelter with a general surgeon, a Captain who had no wife and a deep capacity for warmth.

And they were happy.

She had just gotten off duty, stripped off blood-stained fatigues (one of her patients, dying hysterically, had ripped out his IV and smeared her with the very O-positive-low-titer he had received during surgery), snapped on her reel-to-reel, thrown on shorts and a tie-died T-shirt; she was humming along with Judy Collins, hunting for fingernail clippers in the clutter of hair ribbons and Dinty Moore cans on her dresser, when someone knocked on the door of her hooch.

She opened it, looking for her captain.

Instead, a short, tanned young infantry specialist stared at her with huge brown eyes, deep as the abyss.

"Excuse me, Ma'am," he said, removing his cap, fingering it with small, nervous fingers. "Are you Mattie DeLuca?"

The hairs on the back of her neck bristled slightly. "Yes."

He stuck out his hand. "I'm James Gandy. My brother—you remember David?"

She nodded. "You're David's brother?"

"He said—he told me if I was in Chu Lai, I should look you up."

"He never told me," she said, "that he had a brother."

She let him in, and they sat side-by-side on her narrow bed and talked. Of how David was looking for a job in his old home town. Of how James had joined the Army a year after his big brother. Hesitantly, as he spoke, he reached his arm around her shoulders and leaned toward her, but she sat stiffly, and he soon dropped his hand to the bed-space between them.

He shook her hand. Then he left.

When her captain came for her, he found Mattie crying on her bed. And he didn't understand, for the life of him, why she just couldn't tell him what was wrong.

* * *

"Come on in, Lieutenant. You're all wet—here, I keep a towel in the office here—take it. Can't be too prepared, what with this rain and all."

Reno wiped her face, blotted her pony tail with the olive drab towel, and tossed it back to the private. He draped it over the corner of his desk.

"I need a ride back to Chu Lai. They said maybe you could help me?"

The private nodded, and a smile split his long, black face. "Be honored. You just up for the day, Lieutenant?"

"I came up by jeep with one of the guys, but he's not going back tonight." She nodded at a straight-backed chair in the corner. "May I?"

"Of course you can. I'm sorry. We don't get many ladies around here, so I kind of forgot my manners." He picked up a telephone handset. "Let me call up one of the guys, see what's going down your way."

Reno glanced around the office as the private spoke into the phone. There was one wall with a window, full of rain. The other walls were covered with posters. Directly behind the private was a view of the Arc de Triumph in Paris, and a travel poster of two slightly overweight young women in grass skirts and leis, smiling and beckoning her to Hawaii.

She shifted in her seat. On the wall to her right hung three more posters and a large photograph. Closest to her was Tahiti, where a bevy of island beauties danced among palm trees. Next to that, a grinning

154

woman from Holland's Central Casting, feet in wooden shoes, cradled a bouquet of outrageously-colored tulips in her arms. Next, a stock scene from Switzerland: a pneumatic Heidi amid goats on an alpine slope. And farthest from her, in the corner near the rear wall, hung the photograph, a black-and-white shot, maybe 24-by-30 inches, of a woman standing in the surf, silhouetted against an out-of-focus white beach.

As the private laughed and spoke quietly into his handset, Reno's eyes took in the shape of the photo's subject. It was not the long-stemmed body of a model; rather, the breasts were small, the waist slim and long, the legs short but shapely.

She stood and walked closer, and noted with surprise the cut of the shadow-woman's bathing suit and her hair, dark and long, riffling back softly in the ocean breeze. The silhouetted face—sharp nose, small chin—smiled at something off beyond the edge of the picture.

The private hung up.

"Where did you get this?" Reno asked.

"Oh, that?" He shrugged. "Some guy took it down the coast. You got a ride, Lieutenant. Just go out on the pad and ask for Chuck; he's the pilot—"

"Private, this is *me*."

He cocked his head. Then he squinted from the poster to Reno. "No shit?"

"Yes. That's *my* bathing suit—see this? I have this little ruffle here, and the top's a halter. My hair's down—" She pulled the band from her ponytail, and her wet brown hair fell to mid-back. "And that's Chu Lai Beach. See this over here?"

He walked up to the photo and squinted at her finger, which traced a long, fuzzy building behind the bather.

"That," she said, "is the beginning of the Marine compound." She folded her arms and faced him. "Who the hell took that shot?"

"A buddy of mine," he said. He walked back to his desk and sat on the corner. "He's gone."

She looked from the private to the picture, then back again. "Gone?"

The private nodded. He picked up a pen, laid it over two fingers, watched it dip and balance. "Chopper went down two weeks ago."

"I'm sorry."

He looked up at her. "That's you, all right. Funny, huh?"

"I guess." She pointed at the picture. "I come out here, in the middle of nowhere, walk in, and..."

"Yeah." He clicked the pen once, twice. "There you are, right up on my wall. I didn't know it was really—*someone*, you know? I mean, I figured it was some USO type." He set down the pen, knotted his long, dark fingers together. "I suppose if you want it, you can have it—I mean, it *is* yours, you know."

She touched the poster, traced the shoreline with a finger.

"It don't look like you knew he took it. Don't get the wrong idea—he wasn't the kind of guy who'd, you know, bother a girl, or do anything they don't want—"

"It's okay, Private. It's not a big thing, really. It's just—strange, is all. It's pretty modest, as pin-ups go—"

"He'd just got the camera. Took it everywhere with him." The private closed his eyes briefly, then looked up at her. "I don't suppose I got the right to keep it if you—"

"No," she said softly. "You can have it."

The whine of a helicopter rotor cut through the air. The private looked out the window, into the grey and murky afternoon. "Looks like the rain's let up some. I think you'd better get out there, Lieutenant."

"Thank you, Private. I appreciate this." She glanced once more at the photograph, then moved to the door.

"One thing." He stood up. "This may sound kind of strange, but could you do me a favor?"

She paused, hand on the doorknob.

He looked embarrassed. "Could you sign the poster?"

"I'm not a celebrity, Private."

"No." His round, black eyes strayed to the poster. "I know that. But it'd be...a nice touch." He held out his pen. "In the corner would be good. And just say something like, 'Hi, Stanley.' Or maybe just 'To Stanley.'"

Reno took the pen. "Your name's Stanley?"

"No," he said.

He watched as she signed her name with a flourish. "It was his," he said.

* * *

It started with a game of chess, and progressed to the floor of the hooch, a pure case of fraternization—motor pool fatigues fraternizing with OR blues; sneakers with combat boots; OD boxers with lacy stateside bikinis. And it was good for her. And good, too, for him.

For as long as it lasted, which was exactly three weeks.

Secret fraternization, Lieutenant with E4.

The thing with fraternization is, it is a big no-no in this man's Army. There are no Men or Women here; there are only Officer and Enlisted. Oil and Water. Cat and Dog. Master and Slave. Fraternization leads to familiarity leads to contempt leads to favoritism. No matter that one deals in bodies and one in motors, and the twains meet only on the floor of this hooch; such is this fraternity—within this Army Fraternity—that fraternizing with the ally is the enemy.

Or so it goes in the states, where life is orderly and rank files by, marching to its own drum, *left-right*, and lower salutes higher first, and careful tally is kept as to who walks to the right, and who to the outside, and who's ahead and who's behind.

But this is Viet Nam, where the life of an orderly isn't, where jungle heat renders the files rank, and all march to the drums of the Doors and the Stones. Viet Nam, where Death is an equal-opportunity reaper, at least where specialists and privates and sergeants and lieutenants and captains are concerned (even He dare not touch a scythe to eagles and stars, unless their chauffeured choppers soar too close to the sun). Here, the plate is full; there are other fish to fry. You can't take it with you. Too many gooks spoil the wrath. A stitch in time saves lives. A penny saved must be converted to MPC.

Or so it goes in Viet Nam in general.

But this is the 27th Surg, specifically. Where the war is being Wound Down, given over to the Vietnamese. Where the Viet Nam War is being Vietnamized, as the Brass say. Where Patient Census is down and Spare Time is up; where long, barren, dusty days are turning to long, barren, muddy days. Where the threat of Sudden Death from the sky now vies with the threat of Prolonged Death from boredom to win the hearts and minds of those who simultaneously serve and sit and wait.

So: she didn't care. He didn't care. For as long as it lasted, which was exactly three weeks.

The Army didn't care.

Unofficially.

The Lieutenant-Colonel, however, cares. Officially, the Lieutenant-Colonel cares. The Lieutenant-Colonel cares because the Lieutenant-Colonel feels that discipline is Important. Discipline preserves the Structure. Without the Structure, the Whole Damned House falls down.

And the Lieutenant-Colonel cares because the Viet Nam War in Chu Lai is being Vietnamized and she has the Spare Time and the Leisure to care.

The Lieutenant-Colonel levels her eyes at the Lieutenant, who sits across from her, on the other side of the Lieutenant-Colonel's wide oak desk. "What do you have to say for yourself, Lieutenant?"

The Lieutenant presses her lips together. Then she says, "I

don't see the problem."

The Lieutenant-Colonel sits ramrod straight. Her little grey eyes narrow; her helmet of orderly brown curls bristles in orderly outrage. "You are, I am certain, fully aware about the rules on fraternization. There are reasons for rules, Lieutenant. Discipline is necessary for the whole structure. Without it, where would we be?"

The Lieutenant slumps defiantly.

"I have warned you before, I'm sure you recall." The Lieutenant-Colonel lifts her square-cut chin. "Two weeks ago, I told you about the Combat Boots. And yet, just a day ago, didn't I see you in the Club—"

"I find it very difficult to dance with combat boots on."

"Don't be insubordinate, Lieutenant."

"I'm sorry." Pause. "*Ma'am.*"

The Lieutenant-Colonel crosses her arms over an impressive, impeccable, impassive bosom. "You are out of uniform, Lieutenant, if *any item* of your uniform is missing."

The Lieutenant-Colonel stares at the Lieutenant fixedly, and the Lieutenant stares back.

"Now. What do you have to say for yourself?"

The Lieutenant takes a deep breath. "I wish to request a transfer."

"That's hardly necessary, Lieutenant."

"I wish to request a transfer."

The Lieutenant-Colonel's small grey eyes narrow almost to the point of disappearing. Her helmet of orderly brown curls stands to brisk attention. She leans forward in her oak chair, places a tailored elbow precisely on her wide oak desk, and speaks through clenched teeth. "Transfer approved, Lieutenant. But be advised that I will send you to the *worst hell-hole* in this country. There will be no partying on the beach, because there will be no beach. You will be working back-to-back shifts again. You will *work your butt off.*" She sits back. "That is all. You may go."

The Lieutenant rises, gives a half-assed salute, and steps outside.

From where the Lieutenant stands on the second-floor walkway, the compound below looks grey and forbidding, flat-pressed by bruised fists of monsoon clouds. The first pings of rain spear the tin roof over her head, and she catches sight of the E4 two Quonsets away, hunched, hustling a jeep battery into the motor pool tent.

It had been good while it lasted. It has been over for exactly two weeks.

The Lieutenant holds her head high and descends the wooden steps, rain kicking like bullets at the earth, raising little puffs of dust that will in seconds melt into mud. Rain stings at her face, pelts the lenses of her glasses and smears the grey sky into the brown earth. The Lieutenant smiles, genuinely happy.

PART III

Cu Chi

Prometheus Burned

The Lieutenant laid a hand on Sarah Dinsmore's sleeve. "What can I do, Dinsmore?" she called over the whine of chopper blades and the groans of men.

Sarah looked up from a smoke-blackened arm, where she had just inserted an IV needle. Around them, the emergency room Quonset teemed with broken bodies. "I thought this was your day off," she said.

"I didn't have anything planned."

Sarah brushed a tendril of damp blond hair from her forehead with her sleeve. "Did you check in the OR?"

The Lieutenant nodded. "They said they're okay—said I should check with you."

"We've got it covered, Honey." She pressed a piece of tape over the tubing. "We got everybody triaged, and Recovery sent LaCroix. Chopper just picked up some bodies."

Two OR techs rolled a gurney toward the door. Behind them, a man screamed; Sarah dipped into her pocket and pulled out a metal tubex syringe. She snapped a tube of morphine into it, twisted it into place and pulled the rubber tip off the needle. "It's not as bad as it looks, really—you'll learn soon enough that around here, you get a day off, you take it."

"I don't have anything going. Really." The Lieutenant trailed Sarah to a gurney and watched her plunge the needle into the rubber coupling in a writhing soldier's IV tube. "What happened, anyway?" she asked.

"Word is, a direct hit on an ammo dump. Mortars, I guess. Things blew up and caught fire, both, so all the usual stuff's mixed up with burns." Sarah patted the GI's hand; the sheet was flat where his right leg should have been, and his short hair was fire-crinkled. "Okay, Honey—you'll be all better in just a minute."

She turned to the Lieutenant. "You know, come to think of it, there is something you could do, if you insist. See those guys over there?" She pointed with her chin toward the far end of the room.

The Lieutenant glanced across the field of litters, to the corner next to the helipad door. There, four gurneys stood slightly apart from the main bulk of casualties. The men on them were covered with sheets and hooked up to IVs. "Expectants?" she asked. Expectants—the lowest triage priority, patients who were expected to die.

"Three are. Major head wounds, multiple amps, burns, not much left but a pulse. The fourth guy, Hooker thinks there's hope." Sarah shrugged. "He's a Crispy Critter, about as bad as they get. We had to do a cutdown to get a vein. They're going to evac him to Japan, but the chopper's tied up. So he's waiting."

The Lieutenant nodded.

"Problem is, he doesn't want to go."

A man moaned, a low, ragged sound that set the Lieutenant's teeth on edge.

"So what can I do for him?"

Sarah fished in her hip pocket, produced an extra tubex and handed it to the Lieutenant. "Talk to him. Convince him he wants to be saved. He's gonna go anyway—might as well go willingly." She set four morphine tubes in the Lieutenant's hand and piled on a half-dozen alcohol swabs. "We'll make that your very own little corner of the world. Keep an eye on the other guys. The expectants. They so much as groan, snow 'em. Chart what you give, keep your empties; we'll sort it all out when this mess is over."

"Can I tell which man's the evac?"

"Sure. He's got an eye that works and he talks. A lot."

The Lieutenant slipped between gurneys, dodged flailing hands, stopped once to gently detach the fingers of a soldier who had

164

caught her sleeve. "Mary," a man cried, his voice anguished. Another sobbed. *I'm in hell*, she thought. But it was too late to go back to her hooch and curl up with a novel. She breathed through her mouth to evade the sweet odor of burned flesh.

Three of the four men in the corner lay immobile, heads swathed in gauze with breathing holes over their mouths. The blood-stained sheets covering their bodies rose almost imperceptibly with each labored breath.

On the fourth gurney, the one nearest the door, a soldier fixed one eye on her. The other was buried in a bandage that covered half his head. The Lieutenant pushed her glasses up on her nose and carefully composed her expression to one of unconcern, business-as-usual.

The single eye assessed her. "I know, Lieutenant." His voice was husky. "I'm a dead-ringer for Paul Newman." The corner of his mouth moved slightly, an attempt at a smile.

The uncovered half of his face was gaunt, the hair above it a frizzed dirty-blond. She reached up to brush a strand back, and it disintegrated in her fingers. Her stomach lurched; she realized that the ruddiness of his cheek was not sunburn. "Maybe you should rest," she said. "If it hurts to talk."

"Talk is all I can do." He moved his arm, the one across from her, grinding his teeth with the effort. "Here, Lieutenant, move that sheet a smidgen." The forearm that pulled free was blackened, the hand wrapped fatly in gauze that was stained an uneven brown. He dropped it back on the gurney and closed his eye again. "I can't even touch anything. They wrapped them up so I can't see them. But I know there's piddling little left on either one."

The Lieutenant gingerly slipped the sheet back over the oozing bandage. She pulled his chart from beneath the head of his mattress and glanced at it. "James?"

"Jim."

"Jim. It says here you had some morphine a little bit ago. How's the pain?"

"Not bad." He swallowed. "And that's not good."

"Oh? Why's that?"

"Third degree doesn't hurt so much."

She glanced at his chart again. "You a medic?"

"Just a grunt. Did college, though. Pre-med." He opened his eye and looked at her. "You believe in heaven, Lieutenant?"

She hesitated—too long, because he said, "It's okay. I'm not sure I do, myself. But—" He coughed.

"I really don't know what's out there," the Lieutenant said. "What comes after. I used to think there was nothing at all, but I've come to the conclusion I just don't know."

"Makes sense," he said.

She slid the chart back in place and squared her shoulders. "Jim. The other nurse tells me you're having trouble with...the idea of being sent to Japan. Of surgery. There's a lot—"

He gurgled a laugh; it was a careful, economical effort, and she realized he was trying to keep himself still. "I've done my math, Lieutenant. I got half a head left isn't burned. 'Rule of nines' says that's maybe four-and-a-half percent. That isn't burned." His eye mocked her.

The Lieutenant's mouth went dry. "You can't be sure—there are new treatments every day."

His eye pinned her; she felt foolish, naked. She lowered her voice. "I'm sorry. I know that sounds like the company line. But really, how can you be sure? Science, you know? We just put a man on the moon—"

Again, the gurgled laugh. "I used to argue with the guys about that," he said. "Yank their chains. Told them it was all a hoax. I mean," the eye twinkled, "can you really prove anybody was up there?"

"I suppose not." She smiled in spite of herself. "I've got to admit, I'm more than a little dubious these days about anything the government tells me."

The eye closed, and they were silent for a moment, an easy

silence. She lifted her hand, stopped herself; to touch him would be to hurt him. She traced her fingers over the edge of his mattress.

"Lieutenant?" he rasped.

"I'm here, Jim."

He looked at her. "I want to tell you something, but you're going to think I'm nuts."

"You seem pretty sane to me."

"Doubt that. I'm in 'Nam."

"You've got a point."

He stared up at the arched ceiling and cleared his throat. "I was there, right near the ammo. When it blew. You know?"

"Uh huh."

"Milton—guy with me—got blown away." The eye closed, reopened, blinked several times. "Me, I blacked out, woke up covered with shit—wood, sand, you name it. On fire. I mean, I was cooking. But here's the funny part—" His voice dropped; she leaned closer. "It didn't hurt. Honest to God. It didn't hurt, and—" He swallowed hard once, twice.

"Maybe you need to rest a little, Jim."

He moved his head slightly—not a shake, but a definite no. "I was dying. But it was okay." His voice was thin, dry, in danger of crumbling. "I saw my mom."

The Lieutenant was silent.

His eye sought hers, locked into her gaze. "She said it would be okay."

"Your mother—"

"Died when I was 14." He closed his eye. When he spoke, his voice shook. "I wanted to go. I was ready—"

"It's okay."

His eye opened wide. "No," he said with great effort. "It's not okay." His voice rose, took on a hard edge. "I was there, but Simon pulled me out."

The Lieutenant looked away. A corpsman wheeled a sheet-

167

draped body past them, through the helipad door.

"She went away." His breath caught, then steadied. "Lieutenant?"

She steeled herself and met his eye. "Yeah, Jim?"

"I want to go." It was almost a whisper.

She shook her head slowly. "Maybe it's not time."

"I'm not afraid."

"I can't help you," she said.

He said something, but she didn't catch it. She leaned down to the gurney. "Can't—or won't?" he whispered.

Her heart tripped. "It amounts to the same thing," she said softly.

He fell silent; his eye closed. The Lieutenant straightened and glanced about. The three expectants lay inert on their gurneys, mummy-wrapped, sheets rising ever-so-slightly with each labored breath. The rest of the room had grown quiet, and she realized that nearly half the litters were gone. Some, she knew, to the OR; some to the holding ward. Some—- *Gone. Just gone.* Across the room, miles from her, Sarah sponged a soldier's face. LaCroix replaced an IV bottle. A corpsman cut the bandage from a man's arm.

She inhaled slowly, grateful that her sense of smell had blunted, and turned her eyes back to the man. To the charred, skinned shoulder, the angry blisters on his neck. The bandage on his head, now pink-brown with seepage. She glanced up, noted that his IV bottle was half-empty.

His eyelid fluttered open. "Lieutenant?"

"I'm here, Jim."

"I think this might be the worst way to die." He paused, then added. "Except maybe that Greek guy."

"Beg pardon?"

He cleared his throat. "Chained to the rock."

She stared at him blankly.

"In the story. Guy that brought fire to earth." He blinked.

"Ah. You mean Prometheus? The fire-bringer?"

"Yeah." He coughed guardedly. "That's it. The fire-bringer. Like me. Like us."

"Like you. Oh, yeah. You bring fire. I get it. Interesting analogy."

"Thanks. I try."

She thought for a moment. "But if I remember the myth correctly, Prometheus didn't die. He got his liver pecked out every day, and it grew back at night. Eventually, Zeus or somebody set him free, I'm pretty sure."

"Oh. Right. He got free." He closed his eye. "Then this is worse." he said, very softly.

She said nothing.

"It wouldn't take much. I'm not that big."

The Lieutenant watched his IV, watched the solution drip slowly in fat droplets from the inverted bottle, through the clear chamber, into the tubing.

He opened his eye. "She looked good. Happy. Like she was... before." The pained shadow of a laugh. "Funny thing: she had on my bunny slippers."

"Beg pardon?"

"I bought them for her. For her birthday. When she was... sick."

The Lieutenant nodded, feeling lost.

"Fake fur," he said. "Pink—" His eye, now dull, blinked, then sought her face. "I don't want to die like this. Pain...operations... infections—"

She ached to take hold of his hand; it was what she would do if they were back in the States, if he wasn't so ruined: hold his hand. She shoved her hand into her pocket.

"You could just...give me something—" His eye pleaded with her.

The Lieutenant took a deep breath. "If you're in pain," she

said, "I can give you a little more morphine. But I can't—"

He cleared his throat again, closed his eye. "Fuzzy, two pink bunnies, button eyes. So clear, I could almost feel them—" His voice trembled, trailed away.

The Lieutenant pulled her hand from her pocket and uncurled her fingers. Her eyes stung; she felt winded, as if she had run a marathon. She tipped her palm back and forth, and the morphine tubes rolled like smooth, glass pencils.

"Lieutenant?"

"I'm here, Jim."

"Know any hymns?"

"It's been a long time. Hmm. 'Amazing Grace,' maybe, one or two verses. But I warn you, I'm no Joan Baez."

His eyelid drooped slightly. "That's good." His voice was thick. "Amazing Grace."

The Lieutenant twitched the IV valve, watched the drops pelt through the drip chamber. Quietly, under her breath, she began, *"Amazing grace, how sweet the sound—"*

She watched his eye close. *"T'was blind, but now—"* The red skin on the side of his face softened, and the corner of his lips lifted slightly.

"T'was grace that taught my soul to fear—" His face wavered; she lifted her glasses and brushed her eyes with her fingertips, and it resolved, the eye blinking then falling closed again, lips forming a word, losing it.

"How precious was—" In the sunlight sifting through the window of the helipad door, a small bit of fluff tumbled, lifted above the gurney, drifted down to settle like a benediction atop the stiff, stained sheet.

The Perils of Pappy

Spend too many nights in bed with guys you hate to find next to you in the morning; wake up too often with your head in a vise; in time, you come to give serious thought to changing your life.

First, Soriano swore off booze and drugs. Then she swore off sex. Finally, she swore she was going to improve her mind.

All this swearing took roughly a week. Mind-altering substances went first. She'd never really enjoyed getting drunk or stoned; it was just that every party had the same faces, the same cynical lines and hooks, the same music. Liquor and pot made the sameness easier to handle. She began to skip the parties and drink soda without the scotch at the officers' club; within three days, she found her sleep less fitful, her mornings more coherent. Even her eyesight seemed to improve, the colors cleaner, margins of things more crisp.

Men. She'd been surrounded by them, pressed in and sweated upon by them, for six months here in Viet Nam. Old lovers. New lovers. Potential lovers. Wounded soldiers. Amorous helicopter pilots. Corpsmen who patted your ass as you pushed a gurney past. She turned a newly clear eye on the hospital staff, measured them all appraisingly; finding not one god among them, she stepped away from sex. And discovered, after two days celibate, that the earth had not stopped spinning.

This, thought Soriano, *is going to be easier than I expected.*

The mind-improving thing, though. Here, on this parched and dusty piece of earth in the middle of a jungle, far from ivied brick and noisy student union buildings. That could not be so easy.

Could it?

"Try the USO," suggested LaCroix, who worked with Soriano in Recovery, over midnight breakfast in the mess hall. "I think they have a Programs guy—you know, to help elevate the minds of the savage beasts."

Soriano frowned and picked at the powdered eggs on her plate. They were a uniform, cheery yellow. "I don't want to learn how to weave ashtrays."

"Why not? Everybody needs ashtrays." LaCroix slapped a mosquito on her neck, then took a sip of her coffee. "Seriously, I've heard they've got college courses, too."

Soriano snorted. "Yeah. The army hires professors and ships 'em off to Viet Nam."

"I don't know. Maybe they do." LaCroix chewed her cold toast thoughtfully. "The army's done crazier things than that."

So Soriano went to the USO, and she found that LaCroix was right. There was indeed a Programs guy, and he helped her sign up for a night course in Geography, accredited by the University of Maryland. It was scheduled to start in two days at the 25th Division compound.

The hospital's very own Pappy would be teaching it.

Soriano was surprised by this. Pappy'd never told her he was a professor.

Pappy had a real name, but no one used it. He was Pappy. Because, although he was only 24, he was nearly bald, he routinely thought before he spoke, and he smoked a pipe. He reminded Soriano of her late uncle Victor, a rather dull man who had been a CPA.

Pappy had told her that he had a Master's degree in Spanish. In light of this, the Army had made him an operating room tech.

Once, when she was hanging out in the OR tech hooch— the place on the compound for music and primo drugs—Soriano had asked Pappy if he resented being an OR tech. He had waved away the joint she offered, sucking instead on his trademark pipe. "Not at all," he'd said quietly. "My recruiter told me he'd see to it that I'd go straight into the infantry."

So now, Pappy would be giving his recruiter the finger, figuratively speaking, and presiding over a college classroom in the 25th Division's Education Center.

* * *

The University of Maryland's Geography 101, U.S. Army Division of Continuing Education, Cu Chi area, was the very first real college course Soriano had ever taken. In nursing school, she'd endured Chemistry, and Anatomy and Physiology, but they had been geared down, taught for practical use.

This Geography course bore no relationship whatsoever to the last class she'd taken in the subject, in sixth grade at the Beaufort Harmon Public School in Amarillo. There, she had hunched dutifully over her text and watched old Miss Stroop smack the tip of her wooden pointer on a pull-down map of the world. *Snap*! She struck a little printed pile of coal. *Snap*! A coconut palm. *Snap*! A bar of gold.

No, this was something else entirely.

She sat in a rigid wooden chair, at a rigid wooden desk, in the very front row of the beige, paint-peeling, sticky classroom, the only woman in a class of fifteen, her eyes riveted on Pappy as he balanced his spare frame on the edge of the metal desk and stuffed his pipe. She strained forward eagerly to hear his calm, even voice over the ambient night noises—the rattle of the floor fan, the ping of bugs against the screen, the faint *whump-whump-whump* of outgoing rounds.

That very first night, Pappy taught her that Switzerland, possessing great herds of cows and limited in transportation potential by its mountainous terrain, had turned its tribulations to fair revenue by exporting expensive, compact milk chocolate. This was something Soriano had never thought about: that there were causes and effects for such things.

She fell in love instantly, blindly. Not with Pappy (even with his new air of authority, he still reminded her of Uncle Victor), but with

173

unnecessary learning, with knowledge that wasn't how-to-cleanse-a-wound or how-to-give-a-shot. She fell in love with the Liberal Arts.

* * *

"Well?" LaCroix plopped her tray next to Soriano's and sat down. The mess hall was crowded; word had gotten out that the midnight menu would feature Shit on a Shingle.

"Well what?"

LaCroix tapped her forehead. "Your mind. Has it improved?"

"You mean the class."

"Of course, Your Highness."

Soriano cocked an eyebrow at her.

"Royal Queen of the Celibates."

"Very funny. Ha, ha."

"If the chastity belt fits..." LaCroix forked glutinous, lumpy gravy over an exposed corner of toast. She took a big bite, spoke around it. "The class—any good?"

"It's fucking amazing. You should try it."

LaCroix swallowed mightily. "No, thanks. If the Good Lord had meant me to read books, he wouldn't have given me men." She cleared her throat. "You know, I'd be careful, if I were you. Something's going to happen."

Soriano gave her a questioning look.

"Nothing fucking *amazing* is allowed to happen here," said LaCroix gravely. "If it's fucking amazing, something's bound to come along and screw it up."

Soriano pushed her tray away. "Good Lord. Since when did you become such a cynic? It's just a class. What can possibly happen to screw it up?"

"Well. Ah. You could pull a late-shift rotation. You could get raped on the way to school by one of those nuts at the 25th. The V.C. could score a hit on the classroom."

Soriano stared at LaCroix. "What're you, jealous or something? What brings this on all of a sudden?"

LaCroix shrugged. "I don't know. Things have been going shitty lately. You know. Dinsmore's pilot got shot down last week, and we had that incoming yesterday, and the whole P.O.W. ward's got the shits. We've had three mass cals this week." She stabbed her fork into the soggy toast. "And H. Persey Jewett the Third turned out to be a prime asshole."

"I won't say I told you so." LaCroix was a perennial loser at love. Like Soriano herself had been, a mere week ago. Before she'd dropped sex like a pair of dirty drawers.

"Thanks. I'd hate it if you did." LaCroix patted Soriano's hand. "Sorry. I'm just being a pessimist. I'm sure it'll be great, and you'll graduate with flying whatevers."

Soriano rose and picked up her tray. "It's just a class. I'm not graduating with flying anything; I'm just trying not to flunk."

"Good for you." LaCroix pushed back her tray and stood. "I mean it. Really. And fuck yes, I'm jealous."

* * *

The next week, Soriano sauntered across the 25th Division compound, turning a deaf ear to the whistles and catcalls of men in combat gear. Ignoring the little gaggles of black soldiers who appraised her as she passed. The arrogant, sweat-polished men who leaned against jeeps and cinder-block buildings and followed her with their eyes. She refused to notice their lips curving sardonically around drooping cigarettes, or the way the wired-up street lamps lit the muscles in their forearms, folded casually over bare, hard, dark chests.

She walked right by. The next time, she told herself, a propos of nothing, she would wear fatigues instead of shorts.

She walked into the classroom and took her seat among her classmates. Pappy glanced up from the board, where he was chalking a table of economic figures, and nodded. She opened her textbook. The floor fan sputtered to a halt and the lights flickered out, and she heard the unmistakable *whump-whump-whump* of something bigger, and much closer, than the usual out-going rounds.

Oh, fuck, thought Soriano.

Darkness; confusion. Then Pappy's voice: "There's a bunker just outside the room, guys. Follow me."

The class trooped out, knocking boot-toes into desk legs and tripping over the doorsill. Outside, in the scant glow of a quarter-moon, they found the sandbagged entrance to a bunker and hurled themselves into it, past a soldier who hooded a flashlight beam with his hands.

Inside, in the wavering light of another lantern, Soriano moved uncertainly over the dirt floor toward a shadowy line of hunkered-down football players. Her eyes adapted, and she recognized them as soldiers, bulked up by flak jackets and helmets, seated on a bench at the rear. There was a side bench as well; she dropped down on it and hugged herself.

Whump. Whump. WHUMP. WHUMP!

She flattened her back against the wall. Next to her on both sides, her classmates chatted with each other in undertones. At the end of the line, a man pulled a flask from his fatigue pants pocket, took a swig, and passed it along.

Soriano sent it down the line without a sip.

Pappy's calm, measured voice spoke from the shadows. "I think I can get the classroom tomorrow night. Let's meet then."

"Same time?" said the man who'd produced the flask.

"Same time."

"Shit," said the guy on her right.

"Got a hot date, Benning?" said another voice.

"Fuck you, McNulty," said Benning. There was silence. Then Benning said, "Tomorrow's movie night."

"Shit," said McNulty. "*Shit*. You're right. What's on?"

Someone at the far wall spoke up. "The captain's got

Barbarella."

"Can't we have class the *next* night?" Benning pleaded.

Soriano saw Pappy's lighter flare, watched the flame draw down into the bowl of his pipe. "It has to be tomorrow night." He exhaled. "There's an English class on Thursday."

Silence. Ears strained, tense.

Silence.

"Hear that?" said Benning.

"Don't hear *nothing*," said McNulty.

"That's what I mean," said Benning. "See, prof? We could do it tonight."

"Naw," said the man on Soriano's left. "Man's right. They won't put the lights on for another hour. Those were too damned close."

"Tomorrow," said Pappy.

"Shit," said Benning. "I wanted to see Jane Fonda's tits."

"We could hit the movie, call it a class," said the guy to her left. "Check out Jane's *geography*. Oops," he added quickly, to Soriano. "Begging your pardon, Ma'am."

She gave him a scathing look, which he couldn't see.

An hour later, the compound was still dark. Pappy locked the classroom door and escorted Soriano back to the hospital.

*　*　*

The next night, Soriano ran across the compound in fatigues and jungle boots, clutching her notebook and text to her chest. The heat plastered her shirt to her back, and sweat ran in hot little streams from her swept-up hair into her crumpled green collar. Men glanced up, whistled, kissed the air. "Big-assed soldier," mumbled a black man to his companion, as they leaned against a wall and smoked.

Soriano jogged past them. She raced through the propped-open classroom door and plumped down into her seat.

177

There were only five students there, sitting, waiting. The others, she reasoned, must be out in the open field that served as the compound theater, oogling Jane Fonda's tits. She opened her notebook. So much the better; it would be a semi-private class.

It was odd that Pappy wasn't at the blackboard. He was, in fact, not in the room at all.

It was very odd.

Soriano mopped her forehead with her sleeve and waited. Her classmates flipped through their texts and ribbed each other quietly; the guy next to her doodled absently in his notebook with a ball-point pen.

The hand on the wall clock lurched away five minutes. Someone rose and flipped a switch, and the wall fan rumbled to life.

Five more minutes. "Fucking A." The man behind her rose and picked up his books. "I'm gonna go check out the flick."

Two more minutes.

A bespectacled Spec 4 stepped into the room and cleared his throat. "Class has been canceled," he announced.

"What the fuck?" said the man next to her.

"The instructor's sick," said the Spec 4.

"What's wrong with him?" asked Soriano.

The Spec 4 adjusted his glasses. "I don't know. They didn't tell me." He sniffed. "I'm just a Spec 4. Nobody tells me nothing."

Soriano's heart sank. She stood up.

The guy next to her closed his doodled notebook. "Would you like an escort, Lieutenant?" he asked.

She shook her head and walked out.

* * *

A single light bulb cast a shadowy glare over the beds in the OR tech hooch. Pappy's bunk was neatly-made and quite empty.

"Where's Pappy?" Soriano asked.

Three techs—Wheeler, Merrit and Cavendish—stripped bare to the waist, hunched over a tiny table, cards in their hands. Wheeler, a big man with a scraggly mustache, folded his hand and rose. He grabbed a reel from a shelf behind him and fitted it to the business side of a tape player. "Well howdee-do, Lieutenant. How're they hanging?"

"Wouldn't you like to know," she said. "Where's Pappy?"

"Got bit by a rat," said Wheeler, shoving the tape leader through the slot.

"Excuse me?" said Soriano.

"Last night. Right over there, in his bunk."

Soriano dropped down onto Pappy's bed. "Here?"

Wheeler nodded and turned the take-up reel.

"He got bit by a rat in here??"

"I wouldn't shit you, Lieutenant; you're my favorite turd." Wheeler clicked the switch and the reels began to turn. "He was just lying there, his hand hanging over the edge of the bunk, like so—" He hung his huge hand from a limp wrist—"and this big-ass rat just walked up and took a bite."

"Honest to God?"

"Read 'em and weep," said Merrit, throwing his cards on the table and scooping up the change. "Three fucking queens." He accepted a joint from the dark, hairy man across from him—Cavendish—sucked it greedily, then turned to tap Wheeler on the butt. "Hit?"

Wheeler reached behind him, grabbed the joint, stuck it between his teeth, and tinkered with the bass lever. "Back me up here, boys," he said.

"No shit, Soriano," said Merrit, a slight blond kid with zits. "Shoulda heard him—woke up ugly as a sonovabitch."

"Woke us all up," said Wheeler. "I'm surprised it didn't wake up the whole fucking camp. '*God-damn*,' he said. First time I've ever heard him swear."

Cavendish smiled. "It was a very un-Pappy moment. You know him: you'd expect him to sit up and say, 'Hmm.'" He took a calculated pause, then continued in a thoughtful baritone that nailed Pappy's dead-on. "'I believe that a rat just bit me...'"

The other two men roared. The bass lead-in to *White Rabbit* thumped out of big speakers suspended from a ceiling joist. Wheeler pulled the joint from his teeth and reached it behind his back. "Fucker near took his arm off," he said.

Merrit took a hit. "Cavendish saw it. Big as a fucking pig."

"Grandissimo." Cavendish raised a shaggy eyebrow. "Most impressively big." He shuffled the cards. "Do you suppose you could pass that along?" he asked Merrit as he dealt.

Merrit took another toke and passed the joint.

Cavendish set down the deck. He breathed the smoke in, held it a moment; as he let it out, he pointed the butt in Soriano's direction. "Would you like a hit, Yadira?"

She shook her head. "So where is he? They don't evac you for a rat bite, no matter how big it is."

Cavendish dealt, and Gracie Slick began to wail from the speakers.

Wheeler resumed his seat and picked up his cards. He fanned them and frowned. "Well, they took him to the med ward," he said. "And one of the docs—I think it was Hooker—decided he should take the rabies shots. You know, just in case."

Merrit barked a quick, grating laugh. "Hooker," he said. "What a dickhead."

"And?"

Cavendish sucked the joint, passed it on. "Hey, Yadira—did you know that they give rabies shots in the stomach?" He pulled two cards from his hand and slapped them on the table.

"It's given into the *fat*," Soriano said. "Not the *stomach*. If they have to give a lot of shots, they sometimes give them into the fat of the abdomen. Small needles." She shifted on the bed. "It's not like they stick big, long needles into your stomach."

"Dealer takes two," said Cavendish. "Abdomen, stomach—it's

basically the same."

Soriano gave him an exasperated look. "C'mon, guys. Cut to the chase: where the hell is Pappy?"

"Check," said Wheeler. "So they give him the shot, right? And his throat closes up. But he's in the med ward, and the doc's right there, so he hits him with something to, you know—" he waved his hand.

"Counteract it," finished Cavendish. "But that didn't work, so they had to trach him." He took the joint, gave it an appraising look, and puckered his lips to it. "I'll raise you a buck," he said.

Soriano's stared at him. "Oh, sweet Jesus," she said softly.

"Poor fucker. Thought he'd bit the big one for sure," said Wheeler. "I fold. Shit. I can't win for losin' tonight."

"Is he...okay?"

Wheeler nodded. "Alive, you mean? Sure."

Soriano found herself breathing again. Which amazed her, because she hadn't realized she'd stopped.

"You know, I'm surprised you didn't hear all this earlier today, Soriano."

She thought about it. "We were straight out all day. All those guys from the two choppers—the ones you-all sent us, if you recall."

"My day off," said Wheeler. "Can't hold me responsible." He tipped his chair back. "Pappy." He shook his head. "Poor fucker."

Soriano fought to keep her voice level. "So. Once more, men: *where is Pappy?*"

Cavendish let out a stream of smoke and passed the joint. He absently scratched at a furry arm and leveled his eyes at Merrit. "Are you still in this game, Ejo? No?" He grinned and raked in the pot. "The Poor Fucker, as my esteemed and bearish colleague here calls him," he said, "is in Japan now. Presumably lying abed, being served real food by nurses who wear honest-to-god skirts. Poor fucker, hah. I've been trolling for rats all day, myself, but no such luck."

Gracie Slick sang darkly of white knights and red queens. Soriano dropped back against Pappy's pillow and stared at the glaring light bulb.

"You know the best part?" said Merrit. "The rumor on the street is, he's gonna get the Purple Heart."

He barked his ugly laugh and shuffled the cards.

Soriano sat up slowly. "Shit," she said.

Cavendish looked up at her. "Ah, sweet Yadira. You look like a lady in distress." He scooted over on the footlocker where he sat and patted the space next to him. "Come here and tell Dr. Cavendish all about it."

Merrit dealt to Wheeler, then held the next card out, face-down, in Soriano's direction.

She stood up, walked to the table and dropped down next to Cavendish, accepting the hairy, comforting arm he draped over her shoulder.

Wheeler clipped the last of the joint into the teeth of a mosquito clamp and passed it to her. She inhaled slowly, savoring the heat of the roach, the lightheaded peace of the smoke as it curled into her sinuses and wound down into her lungs. "Deal me in, gentlemen. What the hell." She exhaled, picked up her cards. "Might as well lose my money, since I've already lost my mind."

"Not to mention your morals," said Wheeler.

Soriano looked up sharply, but all three men were innocently perusing their hands. She sighed and knocked on the little table. "Check," she said.

Hope Is the Thing with a Golf Club

After the Bob Hope Show hit Cu Chi, LaCroix couldn't listen to *Have Yourself a Merry Little Christmas* without bursting into tears.

That night, late, after the show, she had heard the song for the first time in the season. It was not to be the last; in the days that followed, it warbled at her from radios, from the reel-to-reels in the clubs, from the P.A. system hooked up to the hot, dry, crowded bays of the hospital wards. And every time she heard it, she cried.

It wasn't the lyrics that got to her. In truth, she was seldom able to follow the words because, when she heard them—whenever she heard them—it seemed she was drunk.

No; LaCroix's tears sprang from simple association, the way saliva sprang from Pavlov's dog, rather than lyrical sentiment.

* * *

The Bob Hope Show came to Cu Chi a week before Christmas. That evening, everyone who wasn't scheduled for duty jumped into a jeep or onto the back of a truck and rode to the far end of the 25th Division compound, to the amphitheater. There, board stands rose in a steep semi-circle around a raised wooden platform. This was the stage, and above it hung a great Christmas-tree-shaped plywood proscenium, draped with strings of colored lights and punctuated with a man-sized red and gold 25th Division lightening-bolt crest.

The sun lay low on the horizon as LaCroix settled herself on a hard bench half-way up the stands, between Joanne Cesak of the Operating Room and Lester Seacrest, the hospital registrar. LaCroix had never seen a Bob Hope show, not even on TV. She had put in a long, too-eventful shift in the Recovery Room, and she was eager to kick back and enjoy a real, Hollywood-style spectacle. She patted Lester Seacrest on his fatigue-clad leg. "We're going to get flat-out, no-expense-barred entertained, for a change," she said.

Lester's long face creased into a grin.

Cesak looked skeptical. "This'll have to be fucking great, to beat that Korean girl band with the accordion player who strips to *The House of the Rising Sun.*"

"Cynic," said LaCroix.

"Bet your ass."

The plank seats around them were filled with men. Men huddled on the roofs of nearby hooches; men hung in the scaffolding supporting the klieg lights. Below, muscular men stalked the stage, strung wires, tapped on microphones, waved signals up to the lighting guys in their caged booth, smacked mosquitoes and scratched sweat-stained armpits and crotches. "Wow," said LaCroix, watching a large, shirtless man rip a length of duct tape with his teeth. "Are we drowning in testosterone, or what?"

"As ever," said Cesak. "Unfortunately."

"Speak for yourself, m'dear," said LaCroix.

The kliegs flashed on, ignited the stage, dulled the waning sunlight. One by one, the techies slipped away.

Long minutes passed. "You know," said LaCroix, "I could really use a drink."

Lester Seacrest drew out a leather-covered flask. "I've got some Southern Comfort," he said.

She wrinkled her nose. "Eeeuw. Honestly, Lester. Nobody drinks that stuff but Janis Joplin."

He looked hurt.

"Ah, what the hell," she said. "Sold." She grabbed the flask and took a gulp. "I thought you guys drank mint julips where you come from." She handed it back. "Or at least bourbon."

"Actually," his Louisiana accent stretched the word into several lazy syllables, "I don't drink much of anything. I just brought this along in case you or Joanne got thirsty."

LaCroix hung her head. "Now you've made me feel bad, Lester. Looking a gift horse in the mouth and all that."

"Ungrateful bitch," said Cesak.

The audience squirmed and chafed. Combat boots began to beat a slow tattoo on the riser planks. Cesak clapped her hands to the rhythm, and others followed her lead.

Suddenly, Hope materialized.

He wore camouflage fatigues and a green beret and carried his trademark golf club. The Gold Diggers clustered around him, silver dresses a-twinkle in the spotlights.

Hope swung the club; hands and feet fell silent, and the crowd strained forward. He grasped the microphone. "Here we are, in Cu Chi by the Sea," he said. A beat. "The V.C."

Applause, whistles.

"Why am I here?" said Cesak philosophically.

"Shhh," said LaCroix.

He followed with a quip about WWII, and a pointed crack about Dean Martin's drinking. Cesak moaned.

LaCroix smacked her on the leg. "Jesus, Joanne. He may not be funny, but at least he isn't stripping."

The band struck up a production number, and the Gold Diggers began to gyrate. "You know," said Lester, "they're really pretty girls, every one of them."

"Too many teeth," said Cesak.

In unison, the dancers yanked off their skirts, revealing silver short-shorts and legs that began at their necks and ended in stiletto-heeled pumps. Cesak elbowed LaCroix. "Did you say, 'At least they're not stripping?'"

"I was talking about Bob Hope," said LaCroix. "Of course, *they're* going to strip. *Somebody's* got to."

185

"Shhh," said Lester, finger to his lips, eyes locked on the stage.

Around them, the men yelled and stomped and blew kisses.

The stage cleared, and Hope introduced Miss World 1969.

The men stared in a silence that was broken, at last, by a catcall from one of the hooch roofs. Miss World 1969 was tall and regally Nordic, all long blond hair, bust and hips in a clingy spangled blue floor-length gown. "Wow," said LaCroix to Cesak. "She looks just like you."

"Yeah. All I need is to lose 20 pounds and get a nose job and new tits. But we are about the same height."

"Shhh," said the man behind them.

Miss World 1969 spoke a few halting, Scandinavian-flavored words, then Hope seized the mike and launched into a spate of jokes dedicated to her obvious gifts.

Lester blushed. "That's really awful," he said.

Miss World 1969 blinded the audience with a game beauty-pageant smile.

Cesak leaned over LaCroix. "It's okay, Lester," she said. "She doesn't understand what he's saying."

The men whooped and whistled.

More Gold Diggers, this time wiggling and kicking in teeny micro-mini skirts.

"Maybe it would be better if Bob stripped," Cesak mused.

Hope toddled out once again, small and gnomish. "Eeeuw," said LaCroix. "I don't think so."

More jokes, this time about the Gold Diggers' obvious gifts.

"I didn't realize he was so dirty," said Lester.

Cesak leaned across LaCroix once again. "*They* don't understand what he's saying, either, so it's okay."

Hope introduced Connie Stevens. "She looks like *you*," Cesak told LaCroix.

LaCroix watched the shapely young starlet shimmy. "You

think so? Maybe if I didn't wear a bra."

Lester leaned forward. "Shit," he said. "She doesn't have one on, does she."

Stevens caressed the microphone and crooned in a sultry baby voice. LaCroix's spirits plummeted. The song was *The Weight*, one of her favorites. The rendition was nearly unrecognizable. She nudged Lester. "Gimme your flask," she said.

As the men around them burst into applause, LaCroix drank deeply, then passed the bottle to Cesak.

Hope lumbered out once again and hit the crowd with a couple of jokes about Connie's obvious gifts.

"Do you mind if I ask for that back for a second?" said Lester, reaching across LaCroix for the flask.

Stevens enticed a trio of G.I.s from the crowd onto the stage, and slithered into *Wedding Bell Blues*. She draped herself around the first man, who blushed furiously, and sang of her love for the oblivious Bill. She snuggled against the next guy, pouting pertly, lamenting her lack of wedded bliss. And on to the next, then back to the first—

"He oughta grab her and fuck her right there," the man behind LaCroix observed. "Shit, I would!" A handful of his cronies laughed aloud.

The sun was gone; the kliegs were up full. Sweat had soaked LaCroix's shorts and cemented her legs to the plank seat. She repositioned herself slightly, careful not to kick the guy in front of her. Lester set his flask in her lap, and she took a sip of the sweet, warm liquor. She felt uneasy, a bit paranoid. And, strangely, like a voyeur.

She took another, longer sip. Stevens left, and the Gold Diggers clopped across the stage, dressed like elf extras in a Christmas porno flick.

Cesak poked her and pointed at the TV camera opposite them. The lens was slowly panning in their direction, and the little red light was on. LaCroix waved a disconsolate hand and took another drink.

Cesak stood up, tall and solid. "Hi, Mom!" she yelled.

"Siddown," said the man behind her.

She plopped back onto the bench and turned to him. "Sorry." She smiled. "I couldn't control myself. I haven't written in months—it was a guilt convulsion."

"That's all right, honey," he said. "You come on down to my hooch tonight, and we'll have ourselves a convulsion of a different sort."

Her smile brightened. "In your dreams, asshole," she said pleasantly.

LaCroix passed her the flask. Above them, great moths flung themselves suicidally against the klieg lights. She shifted on the hard seat, envying them.

Suddenly, Hope reappeared, golf club raised like a scepter. The music hunkered down into a patriotic underscore. "A great man," announced Hope. "A great *American*..." A drum roll.

And Neil Armstrong stepped onstage.

The crowd exploded—wild applause, shouts, stomping. LaCroix put her fingers in her mouth and whistled. Armstrong was a god; a mere five month earlier, he had planted the first human footsteps on the moon.

Earnest, diffident, the big red-haired man looked misplaced onstage, a drowning man washed up on the Isle of Semi-Naked Pixies. "You know," said LaCroix to Cesak, "He's a decent-looking guy."

"Maybe they'll let *him* strip," said Cesak.

LaCroix glared at her, exasperated. "Is *nothing* sacred?"

When the cheers died down, Hope regaled Armstrong with jokes about things he might have encountered on the moon. Cesak leaned over LaCroix and handed Lester the flask.

At last, Armstrong stood alone and uneasy in the spotlight and invited the audience to ask questions.

Silence.

Lester's hand shot up. Armstrong nodded, and Lester stood. "Neil," he said, "were you ever a Boy Scout?"

LaCroix glanced at Lester. His long face was earnest.

"And if you were," he added, "did it help you?"

LaCroix heard Cesak groan softly. She pulled the flask from Lester's big, bony hand and passed it. Cesak tipped it up, then turned it upside-down. Nothing came out.

Armstrong pounced on the question as if it were a lifeline. As it turned out, he *had* been a boy scout. He'd been an Eagle Scout. He declared solemnly that his scouting experience had been a driving force in his success as an astronaut. And an American.

Lester beamed and sat down. LaCroix shifted on the plank seat and scratched a mosquito bite on her knee.

Next to her, Cesak banged her sneakers together three times. "There's no place like home," she said softly. "There's no place like home. There's no place like home."

* * *

Shortly after Armstrong answered the Boy Scout question, after the Gold Diggers had shaken their fringed fannies one last time and Connie Stevens and Miss World 1969 had thrown kisses, after Bob Hope had swung his golf club in a final, dismissive drive, the audience filed out of the amphitheater and back to the war. Out-going artillery, which had remained silent throughout the show, boomed its scheduled warning volleys into the dark country beyond the compound perimeter.

The hospital staff returned to find they had gained a few casualties, and Cesak, who was on call, leapt from the jeep to join those who had stayed behind and missed the show.

LaCroix headed to the EM club.

She sipped her scotch and soda in silence, leaning on the splintered plywood bar, and wondered if any of the local V.C. had been watching the Bob Hope show. God, she thought. What a humiliating prospect.

She downed the drink; Nelson the Bartender stepped up and

poured another.

On the reel-to-reel tape deck on the shelf above their heads, Bing Crosby eased into *Have Yourself a Merry Little Christmas*.

A *Merry Little Christmas*.

LaCroix took a belt of her drink, dumped the dregs on the nearest branch of the club's plastic mail-order Christmas tree, and burst into tears.

Drugs

The night sky was black, starless, waiting for next month's monsoons. Above the hot jungle reeks and the oily stink of mosquito repellent, above the insect musk, the essence of citronella candles on their tall stakes and the ever-present tang of *nuc mam*, above all this, rose the unmistakable smell of steak barbecuing on a grill.

The crowd churned and bobbed and sweated, a thrumming, pulsating beast of night-muted motley—olive drab, hospital blue, white, black, neon tie-dye, Hawaiian flower-splotch. Here there was booze, as always. And potatoes, whole, bulging from their natural skins, un-dehydrated, non-flaked. But it was the scent of steak—real, stateside steak—that pulled the brute to this watering hole.

The steak had cost the supply sergeant 20 poncho liners. Twenty new corpsmen would walk away from Supply with jungle fatigues, jungle boots, genuine U.S. Army olive drab boxers, sheets, blankets, but no downy-soft genuine poly-filled quilted camouflage-patterned make-one-helluva-bedspread poncho liners. They would be FNGs; they wouldn't know what they were missing. Not at first. When they did, it would be tomorrow or the next day. Or the week after that. And the supply sergeant didn't give a shit about tomorrow or the next day, and certainly not about the week after that. Because tomorrow, he would be hauling his steak-filled ass out on the first freedom bird of the day. So let the guys on the boats wrap themselves in the poncho liners and eat canned spam for one night—this was his party, and he'd fry, if he wanted to.

Two husky sergeants, stripped to fatigue pants, flipped the great slabs of meat, and the fire leapt and sizzled and lapped at the dripping juices. Men and women queued, nudging each other. *Steak.*

Doctors on duty elbowed their way into the line, wiping gummed glove powder from their hands onto blood-splattered scrubs. *Steak*. When the first chunk hit a paper plate, it was as if a bell had been rung, and the line snapped to attention. One by one they filed by, flimsy plates held level like communion patens, and to each of them was given a medium rare treasure, doused in a green-flecked sauce.

"It's oregano," grinned the taller of the husky sergeants, arming the sweat from his forehead. "Made it myself."

One by one, the communicants smiled back and carried their precious body-and-blood to the picnic tables. And dug in.

The steak was tender beyond mortal belief, shot with a rare and radiant pink that warmed the anemic candlelight. And the sauce—was ever a chef in France so clever, to dollop this buttery, herbed sweetness on his creation?

* * *

Captain Lester Seacrest, being scheduled Officer of the Day, walked out into the void beyond the hospital compound, on his way to challenge the perimeter checkpoints. M16 in hand, the ghost of a fine steak dinner on his palate, the lanky registrar rehearsed the password as he approached the first bunker –

What was the password?

Ah–

Lester approached. He approached, he approached...but the checkpoint stretched ahead, ahead, ahead in a sudden elasticity of time and space, and the green grass snaked up his fatigues as he plodded on.

He halted and checked his blousing garters. Yes, they were still there, sealing his pantlegs to his jungle boots. So how did the grass get in?

He folded down onto his haunches and stuck his hand into the grass. It ruffled against his fingers like living fur. He could feel it writhing in the wind. In the wind.

But he felt no wind.

He lowered himself to the ground, dropped his rifle beside him and bent his head down, down, his nose almost touching the grass. He watched it ripple rhythmically, slowly, sinuously. He heard it. Yes. Whispering. Soft-soft-softly.

Laughing.

Or maybe it wasn't the grass.

He snapped upright and blinked at the black and starless sky. God, the sky was big. So very big. So very empty. And he was so very, very small. Like an ant. A louse. The nit of a louse. Lester had had lice once, in third grade, back in Louisiana. He lifted his long hand, lifted it slowly, slowly, to his head. Lifted his helmet. Stuck his other hand beneath it, raked his long fingers through his sweat-soaked brown hair. They were back, teams of them. Teeming teams. Teeming, teeming teams. He scratched furiously, then began to giggle.

* * *

"No beer. I'm on duty." Sandy waved away Obermeyer's offer with her empty fork.

Obermeyer dug into his meat and sawed off a corner. "I heard the chopper earlier, when I was bringing the plates down from the mess hall. We got something?" He took a bite. "Christ. This is *heaven*."

"Nah. That was just some clerk coming in from headquarters. A guy Sarge used to hang out with in the states; he came for the party." She glanced around. "The lanterns are a nice touch. Where'd Sarge get them?"

Obermeyer shrugged and swallowed his bite. "Probably the Navy. He told me that's where he got the meat." He closed his eyes. "Fucking Navy. Can you imagine eating like this every night?"

Sandy speared a piece of steak. "I don't know if it'd make up for spending your life on one of those hospital ships. Me, I'd be throwing up prime steak, lobster, all the good stuff. I get seasick." She rubbed the morsel in the oregano sauce. "I didn't know mess sergeants could really cook, did you? I mean, they can scramble powdered eggs and make S.O.S., but this is real gourmet fare. This is kind of like—whatdya call it? Hollandaise? No. Bernaise, with herbs. Subtle, but really tasty."

Obermeyer snickered. "This, from a girl whose mother sends her Spaghettios?"

"Up yours," she said with her mouth full.

*　*　*

Merrit sat on the steps to the O.R. Quonset, staring up at the sky. Damn. It was the biggest, emptiest, blackest pit he'd ever seen. Just like Viet Nam itself.

He dipped into the breast pocket of his scrubs and pulled out a pack of Camels, slipped the matchbook out of its cellophane sleeve and lit up. Took a long drag, held it in until his lungs were crying uncle, then let it out in a slow, steady stream. Merrit smoked like an artist. He had perfected his style over seven years. He puffed out three small rings, floating silver floss in the light from the single bulb over the door. Merrit wondered if all the cigarettes he'd smoked over that seven years would, if laid end to end, reach from the bleak little Arizona town where he'd adopted the habit to this fucking O.R. hooch.

Merrit was eighteen, and acutely aware that he looked much younger. His fine, blond, boyish hair refused to be tamed into any mature style. Back in Basic, they'd taken the clippers to it, and he'd stared fiercely into the huge mirror, praying that, when they were done, it would make him look older, tougher, more forbidding. But what had emerged was a fuzzy dome that had looked as if it belonged to a skinny fifteen-year-old with Dumbo ears and an attitude.

His face was pock-marked with zits, which didn't help. Never mind that he'd had his first butt when he was eleven; never mind that he'd had his first piece of ass when he was thirteen, a fat little Tex-Mex prostitute in Tucson, for whom his older brother and his friends had paid entirely too much. She must've been 25, he thought, and her breath was horrible.

But it had been good; *he* had been good, damn it.

He sucked on the cigarette, let the smoke drift up into his sinuses, blew it out his nose. Inside, he was the Marlboro Man. Outside, he still looked like a fucking cherry.

Which he fucking well wasn't.

He'd dropped acid. Twice. He'd snorted coke. He'd smoked pot daily since he'd come to Nam, where the stuff was good and plenty. Merrit picked a piece of tobacco off his lip and scowled at it. Of course, you do drugs, you develop a tolerance, which was why the steak sauce wasn't doing so much for him.

He smiled grimly. Oh, but he was sure it was doing something for other people. Some other people. The real cherries. He turned his eyes to the sky again, rested his elbows on his knees, held his cigarette between his thumb and forefinger like a joint. Not that Sarge had told anyone what the sauce was. He and Offenbach probably schemed it up as a practical joke. Or maybe Offenbach, being mess sergeant, had just made the recipe up himself.

But Merrit knew. He could tell; you can't outfox the fox. It was a slow, steady high you got from eating pot. It took its time getting there, but stayed longer once it arrived. It'd been maybe an hour since he'd eaten his steak, and he was humming pretty nicely. Not enough, though. Fuck, no; not near enough.

He drew on the cigarette, dropped the butt and crushed it out with his sneaker. He stood and brushed off his scrub pants. Not much of a night, work-wise. Merrit glanced at his watch; nearly 10 p.m., and they hadn't had a patient in three hours, and Lt. Crawford was off eating. Steak. With *sauce*.

He barked a quick, ugly laugh and yanked open the door to the Quonset. That should be good. Talk about cherries; she didn't even drink when she was on duty. Everybody else did, including the surgeons. *Especially* the surgeons. But not Sandy Crawford. Such a self-righteous bitch, Crawford.

Merrit wanted very badly to be thoroughly fucked up. All the time. Now, especially. He could work just as well when he was high; in fact, he could work a shitload better, because he didn't think all the time about the zits and the skinny arms, and how he looked to the dingbat nurses and the other techs, and the whores in Saigon, and his brother Leo, who was a weight-lifter and a champion college wrestler back in the World. When Merrit was high—*really* high, which took a fair amount of doing—he was *smooth*. He was so smooth he was *slick*.

For the moment, unfortunately, he was most un-slick. He was out of weed. Out of hash. Out of coke. And out of money until Tuesday.

Yessir, these were fucking desperate times. And fucking desperate times called for fucking desperate measures.

The light in the lounge stung his eyes, and he squeezed them shut for a moment. Everything was quiet. The place smelled like a hospital, and that smell was charged with angst. And repetition. And boredom. After eight and a half months, nothing's new; after eight and a half months, even the most complicated case comes down to working on a slab of meat. Merrit opened his eyes, sighed, and walked into the storage room. Bloody, muddy, drippy meat. People steaks. The thought made him a bit queasy. He grabbed the nearest anesthesia machine and pulled it to the door. *I have three months, twelve days and—*he checked his watch—*six hours and twenty minutes more of this shit*, he thought.

* * *

Captain Lester Seacrest felt as if he were dragging the perimeter back through the undulating grass with him. The faintest hint of a headache had begun to flicker about his temples. He'd managed to remember the password and to check all the check points, but he'd lost his M 16 somewhere.

He dragged his foot around, turning in a slow circle, trying to touch the damn rifle with his boot. Shit.

Dizzy, he dropped to the ground and tried to think.

He'd had it at the last checkpoint.

Hadn't he? He took off his helmet and set it beside him and put his damp head in his hands. Shit, shit, shit.

Of course, he'd had it at the last checkpoint. He'd been scared shitless that one of those idiots in the bunker would blow him away, because he hadn't been sure that he'd get the password right. So he'd taken the gun and held it, pointed it at the bunker...

And then what?

Lester's head snapped up. He'd been so thrilled to pass the checkpoint that he'd flung himself down into the grass afterward—

Lester groaned. That meant he'd have to retrace his steps. He stood up on legs gone wobbly. Everything around him was black and empty. The dizziness was gone, however. That was good. That was very good. He tried to orient himself, but there were no familiar points from which to orient. Only blackness. He took a few tentative steps; they felt right. So he began walking.

Uh, oh—his helmet. He turned and walked back, bent down, and felt on the ground for it.

It was gone.

Shit. Shit, shit, *shit*.

* * *

Sandy Crawford laughed out loud. She wondered how the hell Obermeyer had gotten so funny. Maybe it was just the way he looked. Like a rodent. He looked like a skinny little mouse, with that long nose, that little whiskery mustache. What was it he'd said? She stood up abruptly and her empty paper plate shifted in her hand of its own accord. "I gotta go," she said.

Obermeyer waved her away and began a new story for the others who remained around the picnic table.

Sandy leaned over the metal rim of a trash barrel and dropped her plate and plastic fork, and watched them float down into the darkness in slow motion. Damn, she thought. How did they do that?

She started toward the O.R. Quonset. And stopped. And looked up. The sky yawned above her, huge and blacker than the ground. She stood gaping at it. Then she looked down at the Quonset. Beyond it was a wide field; she'd never noticed it before. She'd known it was there, but she'd never *noticed* it. *What was out there, anyway?* She tried to think. *The infantry company, was it out there? Or was it*—she swung around, and had to steady herself against a wash of giddiness—*over there?* She glided off in the direction where she thought it might be, but there were no lights. There should have been lights. She glanced over her shoulder at the crowd and watched them grow smaller: the tables, the people, the twinkly little hanging lanterns, and the 55-gallon drums that had been sliced in half lengthwise and covered with wire and filled with barbecue fire.

The funny thing was, they seemed to grow smaller while she was standing still. She laughed.

Suddenly, she smacked into a tree. She tumbled backward.

The tree spoke. "What's that?"

She caught herself with her hands and looked up and up at the tree, which was lean and lanky and tall, and was Captain Lester Seacrest.

"Christ!" she said.

He squatted down. "Are you all right? Crawford?"

"Yeah. It's me. Lester?" She giggled. "I thought you were a tree."

"I think I lost something," he said.

She grabbed him by the shoulder so she could pull herself up. Her fingertips pressed into the damp cloth of his fatigue shirt, into his flesh, to the bones beneath, and it gave her a shivery feeling to know they were there, the bones, with their secret contours. She giggled again. And put her other hand on his other shoulder. There were bones there, too; she felt them through the cloth and the muscle, a hardness beneath the resilient meat. Meat and bones. No fat. She pulled to bring herself up, but only managed to bring him down over her.

And she was puzzled to feel at once vaguely depressed and very sexy.

He touched her chin with the tip of his long finger. It was an awkward gesture, and he pulled it back immediately after it made contact.

But she caught the finger and put it in her mouth and sucked it very, very lightly.

"I think I lost something," Lester Seacrest said in a very small voice.

* * *

Merrit recalled the night of the Grand Porno Review, when he and the guys in the hooch watched those three films they'd checked out of the USO. He smiled beneath the mask. Man. The broad with the superboobs. What was that one called?

Bouncing Betty. Bingo—couldn't forget that one. Just like the mine.

And that little donut dolly that sat beside him through all three flicks, drinking beers and flinging the can tops at the screen. Letting him feel her up. Feeling him up. Joani with an "i" and no "e." She was a sweet piece, was Joani, fat as a muffin. Damn. He laughed out loud, and listened comfortably to the way the mask swallowed the sound, like laughing into a funnel. All his women seemed to be fat. What was it with him and fat women?

They all had big boobs, too, being fat. Not as big as Bouncing Betty's, but round and juicy. His left hand contracted slightly, lazily, palming the dream like a big old softball. His mind drifted, lit on Crawford, who had pretty big boobs and wasn't fat, and would never never never sit through the Grand Porno Review, and he undressed her, undressed those boobs, all very clinically, because he was too blissed to get a woody.

His ma's face wafted serenely through his brain. She was fat, too, was Ma. He made a half-assed effort to not think of her boobs; that was sick shit, thinking of your mother's boobs. Unless maybe you were a baby. He laughed again—*huh, huh, huh*—into the mask. And he thought, suddenly and in living, longing color, of his old, fat, piebald teddy bear.

* * *

Giant fans beat the sky, and Sandy Crawford opened her right eye. Her left was buried; her left arm was pinned beneath what felt like a sandbag. Her right eye saw only blackness. *She'd gone blind.* But no; she lifted her head and turned it toward the nearing rhythmic beat, and both eyes found the approaching searchlight of a Huey. She sat up, and the weight slid from her arm and hit the hard ground.

And bounced. "Ow—son of a biscuit—"

The wind from the helicopter ruffled them briefly, then its light slipped over them. Sandy's mouth tasted as if she'd gargled bug repellent. "Is that you, Lester?"

He struggled upright. "Oh, shit. Crawford."

She leapt to her feet. Her scrub shift was hitched around her waist; she yanked it down, and realized that she didn't have anything on beneath it. "Lester, quick—feel around, see if you can find my underwear."

"I've got to pull up my pants first."

She dropped to her knees and felt around. "Where are my panties?"

She heard him somewhere to her right, tugging at clothing. "I'm really sorry, Crawford." His voice came in little runners' gasps. "Really. I don't know what—"

"Shut up, Lester." She patted the ground frantically. "Shit!" Beyond them, the helicopter dropped slowly toward the helipad. "Oh, thank God!" She climbed to her feet and pulled on her panties. "I'm not even sure—did we do anything?"

"I swear, I never wanted—I mean, I'm a married man—"

"Look, I don't have time for this now. The chopper's on the pad; I probably have cases. Chalk this up—" She yanked her skirt down—"to temporary insanity."

"Actually, I felt a little sick."

She started to laugh. "Geez. Thanks alot."

She felt his hand grasp her arm. "That's not what I meant. Really. I—it's not you, really. I find you—"

"I've got to go. Can't you talk faster?"

"Well, you're pretty."

His drawl gave the word at least three slow syllables.

She roared. Bent over. At last, she straightened up, wiped her eyes. "Christ, you sound like a first-grader!"

"I wasn't going to do anything, I swear to God. I'm married. I love my wife—"

She tangled her belt, retied it. "Lester, this doesn't mean we have to buy a house and a station wagon. Let's go."

He didn't move. "It's just that I lost my gun, and my helmet, and I've been feeling—"

"I'll help you find them in the morning. Are you coming with me, or not?"

"I'm coming."

"Good." She grabbed him by the arm and pulled him toward the sound of the chopper, toward the pinpoint of light that marked the triage Quonset next to the pad. "You know," she told him as they stumbled through the grass, "it's not the end of the world, losing a gun and a helmet."

"That's easy for you to say—"

"Well, think about it. You lose your stuff. So?"

"So?"

"What're they gonna do, send you to Viet Nam?"

* * *

Bright light and tepid air hit them when they opened the door to the O.R. Sandy looked at Lester. "You know, if I were you, I'd button my shirt," she said.

"Oh. Right." He fumbled at his shirt front. "Nobody here yet."

"No." She turned to him and lifted her hand to his cheek; her touch confused his fingers and made them even clumsier.

"Will you kiss me?" she asked him.

"I don't know—"

She stood on tip-toe and pulled him to her by his shirt collar. Her lips were warm, and he found himself responding to them in spite of his misgivings.

"That's good." She said. "That's really good." She gave him a quick hug, then broke away. "I just wanted to see what I'd missed."

They heard the suck of the airlock door that led into the first O.R. room, which was hidden from them by a five-foot partition.

"Hello?" called a male voice. "Triage. You've got a patient coming in five minutes—"

"Coming," called Sandy, straightening her shift.

"What the fuck?" said the voice. There was a moment of silence, then footsteps behind the partition. "Holy shit—Lieutenant, get in here!"

Lester watched Sandy slip behind the partition, then leapt after her when she screamed.

In the first O.R. room, on the narrow table beneath the big unlit O.R. light, a slight young man lay still. Lester watched Sandy and the Triage tech wrench an anesthesia mask from his face. It was a pockmarked face, a boy's face, unnaturally pale beneath the tropical tan. Lester noted the blue cast to the lips, the limp hand hanging puppet-like off the table. He watched Sandy poke her fingers into the side of the boy's neck, and the rubbery resistance of the neck, and the pallor that did not change with the pressure of her fingers.

"He's dead," Lester said quietly.

Sandy stared up at him, wild-eyed.

The Triage orderly grabbed the boy by the shoulders and shook him, bouncing his head against the hard table. "Fucking Merrit," he growled. "What the fuck?? What the *fuck*??" His voice rose. "Fucking Merrit—why the fuck didn't you turn on the O-2?" He let go, his breath catching in a sob.

"Merrit!" Sandy wailed. But there was no answer. She beat on his scrawny chest, but there was nobody inside.

Lester moved to the anesthesia machine and looked for switches. The oxygen tank's switch was off; the valve on the nitrous oxide tank was wide opened. He turned it to "off," halting a gentle hiss that none of them had noticed.

The silence was sudden and complete.

This Rough Magic

Sammy Cohen had magic hands, and because of them he seldom paid for his own Chivas. Sitting at the bar in a club, Sammy would take out a quarter, place it on the back of his hand, and move his finger joints ever-so-slightly. And Hey Presto: the coin would walk his knuckles, neatly somersaulting from thumb to middle to pinkie and back again.

Inevitably, the guy next to him would watch in wonder, then he'd beg Sammy to show him how he'd done it.

He would buy Sammy a drink.

And Sammy would deign to show the G.I. how to walk the coin.

It was, after all, a minor piece of business, and Sammy could afford to be generous because he did it much better than the GI ever would. Also, giving the trick away not only netted him free liquor, it gave him the goodwill of his audience. Were he a superstitious man, he might also have said it brought him good luck. But Sammy didn't believe in luck, although he might give lip service to the term onstage.

Still, whether he called it luck or not, it was a simple truth that the very first time he had given a fellow soldier the heretofore secret insight into what made his quarter walk, it had almost certainly saved his life.

* * *

Sammy Cohen had mastered the coin walk at age 10.

He had bought his first rabbit at age 12. The late Hector, not his finest, but his favorite, because you always love your first rabbit best. Sammy had cried like a baby when Hector had gone to Rabbit Heaven, the victim of an unfortunate accident involving a reclining lounge chair and Sammy's 320-pound father.

Sammy had bought his second rabbit at age 14.

He had bought his first pair of doves at 16.

He had gone on the *Tonight Show* at 17 as Sammy Cohen, Magic Boy, and the exposure—and his slender elegance and dark good looks—had snagged him gigs in clubs and coffee houses all over California.

Then, at 19, he dropped out of Berkeley to pursue his passion full-time.

The Army snapped him up, just like magic. One night, he was sawing his Lovely Assistant Arielle in half in a Fresno nightclub; the next morning, Hey Presto: he was on the bus to boot camp.

When he emerged from his training, a skinny and intensely frightened fighting machine, the Army waved a sheaf of papers and made Sammy Cohen appear as a grunt in the 25th Infantry Division in Cu Chi, Viet Nam. But then *it* happened, that which Sammy wouldn't call "luck," although it might have saved him from a combat death: Two days before he was to march off into the jungle, he sat down in an Enlisted Men's club on the base camp, next to a gruff, sinewy Master Sergeant.

He pulled out a quarter.

Within two days, Hey Presto: the Sergeant had—almost—mastered the coin walk. And Sammy found himself in the Saigon office of the USO, penning a list of magic supplies he'd need sent from home.

The USO Major ran an eye down the list. He glanced at Sammy without humor. "'One assistant?' I'm afraid that's not possible, Mr. Cohen."

Sammy balanced a quarter on his long, shapely index finger. "You can't blame me for trying," he said amiably.

* * *

"Oh, wow, do that again!" DiDi Britten's big blue eyes

followed the quarter as it somersaulted over the soldier's knuckles, then doubled back without a hitch.

Sammy tossed the coin in the air, caught it, showed the woman an empty palm. Nelson the bartender leaned over and scrutinized the hand, his small eyes puzzled beneath a single long, bushy eyebrow.

With a flourish, Sammy pulled the missing quarter from DiDi's ear and held it up.

His small audience applauded, and the bartender set another Chivas down where Sammy's empty glass had been.

"Are you really infantry?" DiDi laid a finger on Sammy's 25th Division shoulder patch, black lightning on khaki. "I can't imagine you out in the jungle, pulling coins out of VC ears. I mean, there's not much call for that kind of thing out there, from what I've seen."

"He could make the VC disappear," rumbled the bartender.

Sammy rewarded him with a small chuckle. "I'm infantry," he said. "It's only because I have to be something; in truth, I'm attached to the USO." He pulled a deck of cards from his shirt pocket. "I've just come off the road, where I played some fire bases. I go back out in two days."

DiDi sipped her brandy thoughtfully. "How long do you go out there? I mean, without coming back?"

Sammy fanned the cards. "Pick one," he said. "I don't generally stay out overnight. It's not very secure. My show takes about a half-hour—" He shuffled the cards and fanned them once again. "Now replace it in the deck. That's it." He closed the fan and set the deck on the bar top, then rolled up his sleeve. "Nothing up my sleeve—" An ace of spades dropped from his cuff onto the bar. The bartender guffawed.

"Oops," said Sammy. "That's not your card, is it?"

DiDi giggled and shook her head.

Sammy tossed the ace over his shoulder. "I don't need it, then. What were we talking about?"

"Your fire base gigs," said DiDi.

Sammy shuffled the deck expertly from hand to hand. "Oh,

yes. We do two or three bases a day, then come back in, so it's basically a day trip, if that's what you're asking." He pulled a four of hearts from the deck. "Was this your card?"

"No."

"Hmmm." He frowned and reached into the pocket of her Hawaiian shirt—gaudy orange and white, opening low on her considerable cleavage—and pulled out a three of clubs. "This must be it, right?"

"Yeah," said DiDi. "I've got a little brother does a trick like that. It's a force, right?"

Sammy raised his eyebrows. "Ah, DiDi. You know my trade secrets." He winked. "Just don't tell anybody."

"Show me how it works," said Nelson the bartender.

Sammy tapped the deck smartly with a long finger. "Sorry. You're just going to have to learn it the way I did—read a lot of library books." He offered DiDi the cards.

She pushed the deck away. "Oh, no. I didn't say I could do it; I just know how it's done. But the coin trick, now. That's a new one on me."

Sammy picked up his quarter and set it on the back of his hand. It walked over his knuckles as if under its own power. "I'm afraid that's primarily practice. But I'd be happy to get you started on it, as soon as I finish my drink." He dropped the coin back on the bar, folded his hands together, opened them, revealing two cigarettes. "And a smoke." He handed one to DiDi.

Nelson the bartender shook his head and stepped away to change the tape on the reel-to-reel.

"About this USO thing," said DiDi. "Do they ever take soldiers on their day off? Or...nurses who sing?"

He lit her cigarette, then his own, exhaled a ring, gave her a smile. "Do you sing?"

"Actually, yes. And play guitar. I used to do coffee houses."

"What kind of music?"

DiDi drew on her cigarette. "Oh, protest stuff—"

"There's certainly a need for that, but the USO might not approve."

"Very funny." She glanced up at the reel-to-reel, which was playing *Green Tambourine*. "Watch this," she whispered. She dabbed her finger into her brandy and ran the damp fingertip around the rim of the glass. It raised a thin, high-pitched ring.

Nelson the bartender had begun wiping down the plywood bar top; he dropped his towel and lunged at the tape deck. He fiddled with the knobs, moved one of the small speakers forward, the other back. DiDi grinned. "It drives him crazy," she confided to Sammy, her finger circling the glass rim. "Done it a dozen times, and he hasn't caught on yet."

She lifted her finger; the bartender stared at the stereo set-up and scratched his head.

"So tell me." Sammy exhaled smoke. "What else do you do, besides protest songs? And driving this good man insane."

"Folk, some country-western. Blues. Judy Collins, Joan Baez. You know, whatever I can sing with a guitar."

He tented his long fingers. "I can't imagine that the Army would let you run away and join the USO."

"I know that." DiDi tapped her cigarette ash. "I'm not stupid."

He raised both hands in graceful surrender. "I didn't mean to imply that you were."

"We get a day off a week. I can spend it however I want: hitch a ride to the pool, go out on Medcap. Or," She smiled at him pointedly. "Maybe entertain some bored soldiers, if the USO'll let me."

Sammy appraised her: A girl-next-door type, but sexy. A well-endowed Doris Day with freckles and a red ponytail.

"Look," she said. "You probably think I'm just some kind of dingbat or something. I really *can* sing. Honest. Hey, Nelson." The bartender turned from the sink. "Can I sing?"

"Like a sparrow," said the bartender. He knit his single brow.

"Do sparrows sing? Maybe more like a bluebird. Anyway, man, the lady's good."

Sammy drained his drink. "I'll tell you what I'll do. I'll talk to the folks at the USO and I'll come back tomorrow with an answer. When's your next day off?"

"Friday," she said. "Nelson, gimme a piece of paper, will you?"

The bartender dug a notebook from a pocket beneath his stained white apron, ripped out a page and slapped it down on the bar. With a sudden stage sneeze, Sammy produced a pen from his nose and handed it to her.

"Ooo, disgusting." DiDi tried not to laugh. "I had one of my own, you know." She jotted her name on the paper.

"Deirdre Britten. Lovely name. May I call you Deirdre?"

"Whatever. I'm on first call tomorrow night, so if I'm not around, I'll be in the Operating Room. Have somebody run me up the message."

Sammy snubbed out his cigarette. "Now, my dear: the Coin Walk. He motioned the bartender closer, reached out and pulled a quarter from the big man's ear and handed it to DiDi. "Here's one for you, Madame," he said with a bow.

* * *

DiDi's hands, gloved and bloody, were holding two metal retractors inside a soldier's belly when Sarah Dinsmore slipped into the OR, and stepped up behind her on her stool. "Got a message from Nelson down at the Club," Sarah said. "He says to tell you, 'The guy wants you to bring your guitar to the hospital helipad Friday at 7. In the *morning*. And wear a miniskirt.' I guess this guy's waiting for an answer."

The surgeon looked up. "Somebody's got a big day planned," he said. "Clamp."

Wheeler, the tech who stood across the patient from DiDi,

slapped a clamp into the surgeon's latex palm. He whistled. "Seven in the morning. Must be one helluva date."

"Tell him yes," DiDi told Sarah.

"Okie-dokey." Sarah tucked a piece of IV tubing under DiDi's blood-flecked mask. "Got a surprise for you—open up."

With her lips, DiDi maneuvered the thin plastic tube into her mouth and sucked on it. "Ummmm. Coke. You hot shit!"

"A present from Short, Dark and Handsome, according to Nelson. I just added the extra-long straw." Sarah held the can up and supported the excess tubing behind DiDi's neck. "He says it's all he can pay you, he's afraid."

"Hmmm," said Wheeler. "Guess that really IS some date."

"Sponge," said the surgeon. "Well? Where's *my* coke?"

"Forget it, doc," said the tech, dabbing his sponge into the wound. "You can't play guitar and, if you don't mind my saying so, you'd look like shit in a miniskirt."

* * *

Men sat amphitheater-style up the stark packed-dirt hillside of Firebase Omaha. Shirtless, sweating in the fiery noon-day sun, they squinted down at the small dusty circle that served as a makeshift stage.

Their eyes followed DiDi as she strummed her guitar, delivering 20 minutes of Collins, Baez, Cohen, and Lightfoot. They nodded when she sang of sitting boozed and forlorn on rain-soaked tarmac, and applauded the pictures she painted of the elusive, shifting Tambourine Man.

Their voices rumbled wistfully with hers as she covered Peter, Paul & Mary's *Leaving on a Jet Plane: Kiss me and smile for me; tell me that you'll wait for me...*

For 20 minutes, it was almost like Madison again, minus the beards and the drinks and the pot. They were with her, and she knew it wasn't just for her flower-printed sundress, the only miniskirt she had brought with her from The World.

It was good, *very* good. It felt like home.

She bowed and a tall soldier snapped her picture.

Sammy took the stage, trim and elegant in neatly-pressed fatigues, dark eyes intense beneath the brim of his boonie hat. She watched from behind the stacked wooden ammo boxes serving as his table as, Hey Presto, he changed a white wooden rabbit into a black wooden rabbit by covering it with a sleeve. She served as his Lovely Assistant Deirdre: she lit his cigarette so he could puff on it, then lose it in his pocket; she picked a man from the audience so Sammy could produce the smoldering butt from his ear; she certified that there was nothing up his sleeve, nothing under his hat—

But magical tricks seen from behind are just tricks. To her dismay, DiDi found that something about his act, his scarves pulled from empty fists and knots slipped from ropes, struck a dissonance. Something amorphous, something she couldn't lay a finger on, slowly drained her Performer's High and filled her with vague unease.

She tried to shrug it off. You never faulted your little brother when he performed, she chided herself. And Tommy was not one-tenth as good as this guy.

But the feeling persisted. As Sammy packed his wooden rabbits and metal rings into a little leather suitcase, DiDi wandered about, shaking hands with men as they cracked open C-ration boxes. A soldier from Colorado thanked her reverently for singing *Jet Plane* because it was written by a guy from his very own state, and held out a cracker mounded with salty canned beef. She took it gamely, a bright smile masking her distress.

The magic wand made it all clear.

It was during the day's second and final gig, on a disheveled piece of fallow ground called Firebase Arnold. DiDi stood behind Sammy, watching with faked fascination as he stuffed a string of scarves into a helmet. Then—

He held his magic wand over the upturned headgear. And the realization struck her, electric and profound, of the gesture's pure beauty. The hand perfectly poised, wrist canted, shapely knuckles precisely aligned; long, sensuous fingers not so much gripping as *caressing* the wand...

The hand rose.

She caught her breath. *Hey Presto.*

The wooden rabbits, the scarves, even the wand itself—these were tawdry props to make lesser beings look like magicians. What had so disturbed her was, simply, that none of his tricks, forces, misdirections or conjurings—clever as they were—could even faintly rival the poignant magic of Sammy Cohen's hands.

DiDi's spirits rose with the wand. She promised herself that—*yes!*—she would someday experience those magic hands herself, on her very own body.

* * *

It took four days for the hospital's Commanding Officer to discover how DiDi had spent her day off. Four days, and she found herself seated in a vinyl chair across the desk from the General.

On the desktop, the latest edition of Stars & Stripes lay open to page seven; even upside-down, she easily recognized the figures in the two photos: the bowing, mini-skirted guitar-player, and the slender soldier lifting a wooden sleeve from a wooden rabbit.

The General was a compact man whose rigidity had prompted the rumor that when the army had awarded him his star, they had also jammed a ram-rod up his ass. DiDi had always found him unsettling, even in the informality of the Officers' Club.

Now, sweat-glued to her vinyl seat, she picked a torn fingernail, terribly conscious of the bloodstains on her scrub dress, of the greasy tendrils of carrotty hair escaping her braid. Terribly conscious of the General's precise pacing—*One, two. One, two.* She felt foolish and guilty, a child summoned to the Principal's Office.

The General halted at his desk. "Lieutenant Britten."

"Yes, sir."

"I don't recall being consulted about this mission."

DiDi's lower lip trembled. Since her very first run-in with authority—in kindergarten, when hunchbacked Miss Rossiter had ruler-rapped her knuckles for eating library paste—the most benign confrontation with those above her on the food chain brought her to the brink of irrational tears.

The General paced. *Right, one-two. Back, one-two.* "Had you given me the opportunity to know of your intentions, of course, I would have refused permission."

"But—" Her voice croaked. "It was my day off."

He halted and speared her with cold black eyes. "Which is no excuse to demonstrate such a lack of judgment." He pulled out his chair and sat down, folding his hands primly atop the newspaper. "You are a nurse. You are a *woman*. What do you think would happen if your helicopter was shot down out there?" He leaned toward her, black eyes narrowed—"How do you think it would *look*? How would I *explain* that you were—" He slapped his palm smartly on the image in the Stars & Stripes, making her jump—"singing at some *firebase*?"

DiDi felt very small, very naughty. Very confused. Nurses flew in helicopters all the time. *She* flew in helicopters all the time. It was the best way to get where you needed to go. "Sir." Her voice wavered. "I could get—" She swallowed—"I could get shot down flying to a medcap—"

"This is *different*," he thundered. "It is *irresponsible*, and you will not do it again."

She burst into tears.

The General gave her a look of astonishment; he yanked open his desk drawer, pulled out a tissue and held it out.

Oh, god— "I'm sorry—" *Stupid, stupid, stupid!* She took the tissue, gritting her teeth. "I'm—thank you. I'm sorry—" *Sorry? Damn it, I had a perfect right.* A perfect right. She buried her face in the tissue and sobbed, mortified, chiding herself for her tears. *Stupid, stupid.*

Then, abruptly. She raised her head, fixed him with swollen eyes. "Sir?"

"Yes, Lieutenant?"

She sponged at her nose. "I've been asked—" she hiccoughed— "Sorry. I've been asked to do a TV show with—" *Hic.* "—with the magician. In Saigon."

"Yes?"

Tears flowed anew. "Next week."

He tapped a finger—*rat-tat-tat*—on the newspaper. At last, he said, "If it's a one-time thing, I suppose I could give you my permission." He cleared his throat. "If you would like," he added casually, "I could give you a second day off, so you would have two days for your mission. If you need it."

She blew her nose.

"But only this one time." His voice was stern. "And no more *firebases*, you understand?"

No, damn it. She nodded wearily. "Yes, sir," she said.

* * *

The hallway in the old Saigon hotel was dingy, its grey walls peeling, its crimson carpet stained and faded to a dirty cabernet. Didi smoothed her sundress with damp hands and double-checked the number on the door: 206.

She knocked.

He was stripped to fatigue pants, his naked chest hairless and sweat-damp, a cigarette between his long fingers. His dark eyes registered surprise. "Deirdre. Come in—I thought you were Darren."

He looks pleased to see me, she noted. As he closed the door, she glanced around the room. A double bed, an old chest of drawers, a flimsy bedside table, a sink. Exactly like hers. "Luxury quarters, huh?"

She smiled. "Who's Darren?"

He drew a pack of cigarettes from his pants pocket. "Smoke?"

"Oh, yes. Thanks." She perched on the bedside.

He struck a match, held it out. "Darren. The cameraman."

"Oh, god. Yes." She giggled. "The fat guy—the one who tried to hit on me."

Sammy sat down beside her, at a careful distance. He placed the room's single luxury—a large fluted crystal ashtray—on the bed between them. "Did he."

She nodded. "He was really kind of sweet. He asked if I'd like to see the sights of Saigon tonight with him."

"Then he tried to hit on me, too. Because that's what he asked me."

She watched him turn his cigarette, honing the ash to a perfect point against the crystal. "Oh. Are you going?"

He shrugged. "I don't know. Probably not. I've been here several times, so the sights have lost their charm. Plus, I can't go to a bar without—"

"Performing?" She gave him a wry grin. "The Great Sam Cohen actually needs down time, huh? Like us mortals?"

He smiled briefly. "Even God rested one day." He rose, walked around the foot of the bed to the room's small window. "Actually, I *am* a little tired."

She took a quick puff, then ground out her nearly-unsmoked cigarette in the big ashtray. "I'm beat, myself. I was surprised how exhausting it is, repeating a song over and over like that. I don't know if I'll ever be able to do *Leaving on a Jet Plane* again." She moved the ashtray to the bedside table. "You know, it's funny: I've caught those little two-minute spots now and then on TV, but I never realized what went into them. And you—you were there twice as long, with that scarf thing. But you looked as...new at it the last time as you did the first."

Stop chattering, idiot.

Sammy said nothing; he stared out the open window into the

growing darkness, smoking his cigarette.

"How do you do that so well, keep it fresh, after you've done it a million times?"

"It just happens. But it's better with a real audience." He flipped his cigarette butt out the window and propped his elbows on the sill. A large bug zagged in past him, but he took no notice. It whirred around the light bulb over the sink, banged twice against the wall and fell to the floor.

She laughed. "God, a freaking helicopter."

"Beg pardon?"

"Nothing." She giggled. "It's just, a bug the size of a football just committed suicide over your sink." She stretched out on his bed, tipped her face up to watch the ceiling fan. The paddles groaned and dragged their shadows over the cracked ceiling.

He turned and looked at her.

DiDi patted the space next to her. "Come on over," she said. "I don't bite."

He stood poised, left hand on the window sill, dark eyes unreadable. Outside, brakes screeched and someone shouted in Vietnamese.

"Seriously," she said, fluffing out her hair on the threadbare chenille spread. "I won't attack you."

Unless you want me to.

He moved to the bed. Carefully, lightly, he sat with his back to her and bent to unlace his boots. DiDi's eyes traced the slant of his shoulders, watched the muscles in his back work, noted the slight curl of black hair at the nape of his neck. From behind, Sammy could have been a boy of sixteen.

He lay back next to her and crossed his arms over his chest.

The silence felt new, awkward. She said, "You come here a lot, you say. To perform?"

"Pretty much. At the clubs and USOs. I also do an orphanage that some Air Force guys adopted here."

"That must be tough, what with the kids not speaking English and all." She turned slightly in his direction, aware of his closeness, aware that his knee was lightly touching hers. He smelled faintly of shaving lotion and deodorant.

Even his sweat smells clean.

"Tough? Not really," he said. "Magic is—universal. It doesn't really need a translation."

True.

"You know," she nodded toward the ceiling fan, "That thing falls, we'll be shredded like cole slaw."

He raised his eyebrows in mock horror. "I suppose today's performances will then be aired posthumously. Our memories will linger on, courtesy of AFVN-TV."

DiDi laughed. "Terrific," she said. "My last performance will be a two-minute spot between *Gunsmoke* and *The Beverly Hillbillies.*"

"In Memoriam." They both said it simultaneously.

"Jinx!" cried DiDi.

"Beg pardon?"

She lifted herself up on one elbow, facing him. "When two people say something at the same time, there's this ritual you go through."

He looked at her blankly.

"You've never heard of that? God—maybe it's just girls do it. You hook pinkies, first—" She picked his hand off his chest, hooking her pinkie around his.

long and perfectly shaped

"Then you do something else; I can't remember what, exactly—" She hesitated—

Please

—then leaned down and kissed him on the mouth.

He responded slowly, at first, then deeply.

Oh, god.

DiDi's heart pounded in her ears. She drew back, trailing red tendrils over his face and neck.

Sammy touched her cheek with long, strong fingers. Then he sighed. "Deirdre," he said softly. "This isn't going to work."

Her heart stopped. "Why not? I mean, what do you mean?"

"I can't do this. Not that I wouldn't like to. I just—" he shrugged, refolding his arms—"can't."

She lay back down next to him. Tears stung her eyes; she stared hard at the ceiling to keep them at bay.

Stupid. Stupid, stupid, stupid.

She pressed two fingers against her eyebrows.

The fan rumbled around once, twice, a dozen times.

"Look," she said. "I know we don't know each other well, but that's not—"

"It's Arielle," he said.

She paced her breathing, calmed it, evened it out. "You're married." The word tasted of salt.

"No."

"Engaged, then."

"No. Not exactly."

"Lovers?"

"Well—not exactly. Yet. I mean, I—we—we'll do all that; we *will* get married. Eventually. I'm sure."

She swallowed. "You don't sound sure."

Sammy sat up abruptly and looked down at her. "I haven't asked her. Not yet. But that's just a *formality*."

She stared at him. A *formality*.

"Arielle's my assistant," he said. "She's the girl I saw in half. The one who helps with my illusions. Like you did last week. But real illusions: real rabbits and doves, boxes with swords through them. That sort of thing."

"And you're going to marry her."

He fumbled out his cigarette pack, shook out two, handed her one. "Yes. Eventually. We've known each other since we were kids.

Since I got my first rabbit. She's perfect." He lit her cigarette, then his own. "The perfect assistant. Would you mind—the ashtray?"

DiDi pulled herself into a sitting position. It took considerable effort; her body had grown rock-heavy. She smoothed back her hair, then dragged the fluted crystal dish to the bed.

He arranged it between them. "Where was I?"

"Arielle." She inhaled, held the smoke in, let it out as evenly as she could. "The perfect assistant."

"Well, yes." Sammy stood, walked to the window, hooked a hand on the sill. "If you saw Arielle, you'd understand. She's beautiful. Tall, thin, long blonde hair, absolutely beatific smile."

DiDi savored the bitterness of the smoke. *Tall, thin, blonde, beatific.*

"You know how the magician's assistant dresses in slinky gowns—-sequins, spangles—Arielle looks wonderful in that sort of thing. I've never seen a girl who looks more appropriate."

DiDi lifted her head at this. *Appropriate.*

"The audiences love her."

"Do *you* love her?" she said softly.

"Beg pardon?"

DiDi cleared her throat. "I asked, do you love her?"

"Arielle?" He gazed out the window, eyes dark and intense.

She inhaled. "I mean, if you're going to marry her—" the words seeped out with the smoke—"you love her. Right?"

Sammy Cohen leaned against the window frame, cigarette between his lips, and stared into the Saigon night. The noise of the street—horns, sputtering moped engines, voices laughing and calling in Vietnamese and English—filled the room. At length, he turned to DiDi, met her eyes through heavy air laced with long curved shreds of smoke.

She watched him pull his shoulders back, arrange his lean body in that characteristically elegant pose. Watched him lift a beautiful hand, two long fingers extended, to remove his cigarette from his

mouth. "We get along very well," he said. "We're perfect together."
He walked decisively to the bed, reached down, crushed his cigarette
butt into the ashtray. "I think I might go out, after all," he said. "You
can come along if you'd like. It's—" he glanced at his wristwatch—
"nearly eight; we'll go find Darren. He's probably still at the studio."
He moved—flowed—to the closet in the corner and opened it. Inside,
DiDi saw his shirt on one hanger and his undershirt on a second.

Perfect. She rubbed her cigarette hard against the crystal
bottom of the ashtray, making a furrow in the debris. A chill lifted the
hairs on her bare shoulders. She crossed her arms and it passed. She
pushed herself off the bed. "I think I'll go to my room," she said. "Like
I said, I'm beat."

"Suit yourself." He pulled his undershirt over his head. "The
invitation is sincerely tendered."

"Thanks anyway." She walked to the door.

He lifted the hanger with the shirt from his closet. "Really."

She nodded. "It's okay, Sam. I believe you."

DiDi flipped the switch and her own ceiling fan lumbered
to life. The dim hallway light bled through the transom and flickered
across its rotating blades. But it didn't reach down to her; in darkness,
she unzipped her dress and let it drop. She pinched the fine stretchy
lace of her panties between thumb and forefinger, lowered them,
stepped out of them, left them on the floor.

In darkness, she touched the tired chenille bedspread. She
pulled it to the bottom of the mattress and climbed in. The sheet was
soft, very thin, laundered to death. She pulled it up to her shoulders.

Lying on her back, she traced the fullness of her breasts with
her left hand. She moved her right hand down, over the gentle hill of
her stomach, to the ridge of bone, into the soft wiry triangle of hair.
Her fingers worked slowly, rhythmically, and as she grew warm and
slippery beneath them, she thought of Sammy Cohen's hands—the
shape of them, the clean, strong, long fingers, the deft and knowing

and poetic grace of them.

Hey presto.

DiDi Britten began to cry.

* * *

Nelson set the drinks on the bar and raised his single furry eyebrow. "That it, ladies?"

Sarah Dinsmore took a sip of her wine. "Nectar of the Gods, Honeybuns." She winked at him.

"You okay?" he asked DiDi. He knew she'd take that to mean her brandy. Probably just as well.

She nodded. "Yeah, fine."

Nelson's heart was all knotted up these days about little Red. She hadn't been herself at all for a week or so. She'd lost her zip, her bubble.

But what could he do? He was just an enlisted guy.

He turned back to the TV set, arms folded over his wine-stained apron. There was Goldie Hawn (cute, but not enough meat on her bones). And the Nazi, tree branches tied to his helmet, crouched behind a park bench. He liked that guy. The sound was pitched low, but after you'd seen an episode a dozen times, you pretty well knew what they were saying.

"Veddddy INteresting," said Sarah, behind him.

"But Schtoopid," DiDi added listlessly.

Guess they'd seen it a dozen times, too. *Maybe what we need here*, thought Nelson, *is a little surprise from stateside.* He reached under the counter and pulled out a jar.

A month ago, that crazy motherfucker Shebak had written a letter to this company that made pickled kielbasa. Seems the bars back home where he came from had the stuff, and he missed it. So he'd gived them a song and dance, Shebak had, about how here he was, poor grunt, fighting in 'Nam, all this death and danger and no pickled kielbasa. Well, damn: just this afternoon, a chopper evacs in a whole fucking carton of the stuff, for free.

Joke was, Shebak was a supply sergeant; the most dangerous position he'd ever been in was under that big blonde from the OR. Nelson pried the lid off the jar and set it in front of the nurses. "On the house," he said.

DiDi's big eyes grew round. "Oh, wow!"

Sarah wrinkled her nose. "God. That looks like something from the OR dump."

DiDi plunged two fingers into the brine and pulled out a sausage. "Pickled kielbasa!" She took a bite. "Oh, god—that's *great*! I used to eat these in the bars at school, up in Wisconsin. This is *heaven*." She rewarded the bartender with a smile. "Nelson, I could just *kiss* you."

He felt himself blush and lowered his eyes—but damned if they didn't fall right on the cleavage peeking out of that Hawaiian shirt of hers, so he ducked down and grabbed a towel off the shelf. "I guess you'll have to kiss Sergeant Shebak first," he said gruffly. "He's the guy requisitioned it." He moved down a space to wipe the bar, although nobody'd sat there for the past fifteen minutes.

When he caught the high-pitched feedback noise, Nelson's heart rose. Damn, she was coming back. He dropped his towel, reached up, played with the TV knobs, and rearranged the speakers he'd hooked up to the set. When it stopped—as he'd known it would— he smiled to himself, although nobody could've told it from his face.

He stepped back to check out the program. Laugh-In was gone; in its place, some skinny fucker was pulling a scarf out of his clenched fist. He looked familiar—

"Ladies?" said Nelson. "Isn't that that *guy*?" He poked a huge finger toward the screen. "Look. It *is* that guy."

The two women looked up. The soldier tucked the scarf back into his hand, then turned an empty palm to the camera.

Sarah grabbed DiDi's arm. "It *is* that guy," she said. "What's-his-name—-the guy that taught you that coin trick? The one you went out to sing with?"

"Sam."

The scarf the magician now pulled out was hitched to a second, which was hitched to a third. Yeah. The quarter guy. Nelson had practiced for hours, days, even; still couldn't keep that quarter from falling off the last knuckle.

"I thought he was cute," Sarah said. "Kind of skinny, but great hands." She was quiet for a moment, then said. "Hey, he made this when you made yours, right? What's the scoop?"

Nelson had seen Red's little film three or four times. Great voice, good song, *Leaving on a Jet Plane*. Terrific legs in that mini-skirt. Flesh on them. Not like Goldie Hawn.

"Thumb tip," DiDi said.

"What do you mean?" said Sarah.

"He does that with a thumb tip," said DiDi. "It's like a fake thumb that fits over his real one. The scarves are really thin, and he scrunches them inside; then he sticks it on his thumb and you can't tell the difference unless he screws up. Which he won't."

Nelson squinted at the magician's thumb. Damned if he could see it.

Sarah's voice dropped low. "I'm not asking about the trick, Honey. I want to know about those *hands*."

Nelson picked up a wet glass and cocked his ears. He wanted to know, too. He sent up a quick, silent prayer that no one else would come wandering into the club.

DiDi sighed like the weight of the world was in it. "He was engaged."

"So?"

"No future in it, you know? Besides." Nelson strained his ears, his eyes following the man on the screen as he stuffed the impossible string of scarves into his fist. "He was a little...crazy."

Sarah said, "How so?"

"Just was."

The guy opened his palm to show that the scarves had vanished. Nelson wondered if this craziness was what had taken such a toll on his favorite lady. He jammed his towel savagely into the glass. He'd really liked the guy. But if he'd hurt little Red, Nelson would be perfectly willing to feed the little fucker his ass.

They watched, in silence, as the magician took his bow. DiDi lifted her brandy toward the screen. "To Sam," she said.

Sarah raised hers. "To Sam."

DiDi took a sip and said something under her breath.

"Huh?" said Sarah. "What was that?"

"Oh, nothing."

Nelson had heard what she'd said, all right; as he always said, he had 20-20 hearing. He frowned, set down the glass and picked up another.

She'd said "In Memoriam." It puzzled him, because that's what you say when somebody's dead.

As he watched Matt Dillon stride down a dusty street, it dawned on Nelson that maybe the quarter guy had got shot down in a helicopter or something.

Aw, Jesus.

He glanced at the girls.

Poor fucker. That would explain why, even with that little smile on her face, little Red's big, soft eyes looked like they just might burst into tears.

Psychic Hand

I had just splashed a little whiskey into my coffee and lit up a cigarette when I heard the knock. Nobody knocks around here—not on hooch or latrine doors, if they have them, and certainly not on the door of the Operating Room lounge. So it had to mean trouble.

I was not up for trouble; I'd had a day of it already. My last work day in Viet Nam, and I'd wasted six hours of it on a fucking Harley Hooper Miracle Marathon.

Magazines on experimental surgery are Hooper's pornography; he's drooling to try all the new positions. He's been a surgeon maybe three years; back home, he'd be grafting extra heads on dogs. Here, he's the star of his own hoary drama: *Supersurgeon versus The Grim Reaper.*

Today, it was a kid whose leg was festering with gangrene, already gone systemic. A septic amputation in the Isolation Room, co-starring Wheeler and me. He tied us up for four hours, while surgery that might actually save someone went on in two other rooms. Of course, the poor sonovabitch died, and Wheeler and I had to disinfect the room, dispose of the gore, change every stitch of our clothing, and wash ourselves down with Phiso-hex.

So I had reached my bullshit limit. It was quiet; I had dismissed everybody to grab some sleep while they could; Jack Daniels and I were purging the stench of Hooper's Folly with a Camel. And some asshole came knocking at the door.

Happy Last Day in Hell, soon-to-be-ex-Lieutenant Joanne Cesak.

I flipped on the outside light and opened the door, and what

225

to my wondering eyes should appear but two MPs and one tiny little Vietnamese woman who might've been 16 years old. "Let me guess," I said. "Trick or treat."

They were not amused. It seemed that the cops—this tough, hairy little fireplug sergeant and his string-bean assistant—had been referred to me by the Officer of the Day. He'd told them I was a woman, and I wasn't busy.

I agreed that I was indeed a woman, and stuck out my D-cups as proof. As for not being busy, I assured them it was a temporary condition. The sergeant asked if they could come in; it was not a yes-or-no question, so I stood aside.

We traded formal introductions, and the long and lanky Private McArthur explained in the thickest Texas accent this side of Dallas that he had found this girl wandering the compound. She spoke enough English to tell him she was looking for her boyfriend, but not enough to give him a name. For this bit of suspicious *bidness*, the private had hauled her off to Sgt. Minelli. Who brought both of them to me.

"Why me?" I asked.

"It's this way, Lieutenant," mumbled Sgt. Minelli through his black mustache. "She's got to be searched."

With great patience, I explained to the men what an Operating Room is for, and reminded them that there was a war going on. I told them I had been here 14 hours, it was my last work day, and I was *too fucking short* to strip-search a gook.

But Minelli was a by-the-book guy; the book said they had to do a cavity search, and I was the only one around this time of night to do it.

"It's not my problem," I said.

But then Pvt. McArthur turned his Texas-sized puppy-dog eyes on me and played on what was left, after a year here, of my sense of decency. This being *The Nam*, he told me, no one would think twice if the men were to do it themselves. "But that idn't proper, Ma'am," he said.

What could I say. Call me a sucker for tall, skinny guys with accents and morals, but I scratched out my cigarette, picked up my coffee and poured another for the little gook. I spiked hers, too; considering how far I was expected to get on our first date, I felt I should at least stand her a drink. I tipped the bottle toward the Boys, but they declined; the book said they weren't allowed to drink on duty.

"Neither am I, gentlemen," I said, as I gave my coffee a finger more. "Neither the fuck am I."

So, for the second time that day, I found myself in Isolation, the only room in the suite with a door that I could close. This time, instead of watching a kid die of Advanced Medical Intervention, I faced a Vietnamese teenager who, even without a BA in English, had certainly figured out what I was supposed to be doing to her.

She was pretty, in a Vietnamese sort of way. Her hair fell to her waist, and under her black pajamas I could see she had a sweet little figure: thin, small boobs, little round butt. She was no taller than my armpit, and she was shaking in her sandals and eyeing me as if I were a hostile Amazon warrior. Which is probably what I looked like, considering I'm nearly six feet tall and built, as one of my high school boyfriends once delicately put it, like a Brick Shithouse.

"What's your name?" I asked her.

Either she didn't understand, or I'd scared her silent. I pointed to myself. "Joanne," I said. "*My—name—is—Jo-anne.*" I pushed aside the towel I'd hung over the window on the Isolation room door and showed her the MPs. They sat at attention on the couch, a pair of ill-matched watchdogs primed to pounce, should this miscreant bite me on the knee. The girl's eyes followed my finger as I pointed, first, to the Sergeant—"*Mutt*," I said—then to the Private. "*Jeff.*"

I replaced the towel and pointed at her.

"Phuong," she said, so low that I made her repeat it.

Phuong. I sat on the operating table and patted the space beside me. "Up, Phuong," I said. She just stood there, her eyes wary.

So I took a sip of my drink and held hers out.

She took the cup with both hands, watching me like an owl; when she drank, she made a face—*Wow, that's Some Good Coffee.*

Again, I patted the table. This time, she climbed up beside me, her eyes never leaving my face.

Silence is a vacuum, and I filled it with prattled good intentions. I assured her I wouldn't touch her; I assured her I was *too fucking short* to play petty war games. But small-talk is no assurance for someone who doesn't speak your language, particularly when that someone suspects you're going to subject her to an unnatural act. By the time I stumbled into silence and dove back into my drink, she had shrunk to the end of the table and was staring at me, the eyes over her cup feisty with terror.

I glanced at my watch; the hands seemed to be stuck. We had to spend maybe five minutes together, if I wanted to convince the Boys that I'd saved the 12th Evac from a ball of exploding shit. I was about to launch into *Five Hundred Bottles of Beer on the Wall* when I struck upon an idea.

My mother, who was born in Poland, reads palms. She's quite good; when I was young, before Dad died and she had to work to support my sisters and me, she had collected a small clientele—neighbors and relatives, mostly—who came to her for readings. She taught me a few fundamentals, enough to keep my high school classmates amused. I was no Nostradamus, but I knew the technical shit.

I hadn't read a palm since I'd joined the Army; I hadn't had time to think about it. But now, I had five long minutes to kill. I grabbed Phuong's hand and turned it palm-up. She lowered her cup and glared at me, but she didn't pull away.

I noticed right away that hers was no ordinary hand. It was a classic Psychic Hand: smooth, tapered fingers with pointed tips, elegant little thumb. My mother would have been over the moon; she once told me that the average reader sees maybe one or two in a lifetime, if she's lucky. Psychic Hands denote philosophers, prophets, poets and saints. Behold: Sister Mary Phuong. Patroness of the Missionary Position.

I lifted her pinky by the tip, noted an almost imperceptible crook in it. "This means you're not entirely honest," I told her.

"Hmmm—*do* you have a rocket up your butt?"

She didn't answer, but she did seem to relax a bit. I guess she'd decided to humor me.

I snapped on the over-table light so I could examine her lines. I checked her right palm, then her left, and my stomach dropped into my bloody sneakers.

My mother always warned me never to predict death; she claimed only God could say when our lives were over. But if these Life lines had been any shorter, I would have been giving this kid artificial respiration on the spot.

Spot. That was another thing: she had one on her right palm, at the end of the Life line. A tiny black spot. I spit on my finger and rubbed it—kid looked like she thought I was nuts—but it was part of her, as surely as the line itself.

Death by violence. My own hands began to sweat; I wiped them on my skirt and glanced at my watch. The hands had barely moved. I didn't know whether to be pissed or thrilled by that. Part of me wanted to halt this nonsense *now*, but the rest of me was pinned. Titillated. Wanted to know more.

I would find her Line of Fate, I told myself; it had to be more promising than her Life line.

But there was none of any consequence in either palm.

God. I was spooking myself. "It's all bullshit," I insisted, and Phuong cocked her head as if to think about that. I smoothed my hand over her palm and looked for something less threatening.

Her Mount of Venus was cross-hatched: a rough life. *Quelle Surprise.* I considered this hypothetical "boyfriend" she'd hypothetically gone to meet, and wondered if he was anybody I knew. Did she fuck him to earn her daily bread? Or maybe she just planted rice, plowed with a buffalo, shit in the paddies and drank the water. A rough life. Okay. Like it takes a palmist to figure that one out.

How old was she, really? Sixteen? twenty, fifty? I asked and she didn't answer. I considered playing Circus Horse, stomping out years with my hoof, but I didn't want to scare the shit out of her. So I moved to her lines of Union.

There was one, very low, almost touching the Line of Heart. She had had one marriage, or one main love, a soul mate, very young. "Aha: he left you for a younger woman," I said. "A twelve-year-old." I laughed at my own joke, and she looked at me as if I'd lost it. Which I guess I had. "Tough audience here tonight, gang," I raved. "I'm *dyin'* up here."

Oops. Sore point, under the circumstances.

I rubbed my eyes, opened them, glanced around at the familiar objects, the flotsam and jetsam of this lost year in my professional life. The little table with folded towels, the rack of tape spools, the step stool I was too tall to use, the mayo stand. I found myself staring at a blood streak on the wall, behind the metal rack with the basin. How had we missed that this afternoon? What else did we miss? Little colonies teeming with bacteria—gangrene, pseudomonas, staphylococcus? I shivered.

Ah, Phuong. She probably believed in dragons. While I, the quintessential Pragmatic Woman, believed in lethal monsters so small they couldn't be seen. But maybe she did, too; maybe she believed in the peril of the unsee-able. Maybe Buddhism—or Cao Dai, or Hindu, whatever the fuck—taught her what the Bible taught me, that destruction, devastation, plagues and runaway buses all sprang from the whim of some invisible power.

Religion isn't much different from microbiology.

Ah, whiskey philosophy. I checked my watch: two more minutes. So I concentrated, once again, on her hand.

There were three little lines at the base of her pinky: three kids. "Babies?" I asked, and I did a little rocking pantomime, then leveled my hand as if on the head of a small child. Her eyes lit up. She smiled, and I was warmed by it; it transformed her face. She was a five-year-old herself, with that smile—sweet, innocent, not the sort of kid who might harbor weaponry in her private parts. I held up one finger, two, three; she shook her head and held up one. I took her hand and looked closely. One line was strong and angled. A girl. The other two, straight Boy lines, were very light.

I set her hand down, grateful that we weren't able to discuss absent boy children. As I knocked back the rest of my drink, there was a rap on the door, and Sgt. Minelli called in to ask if everything was All Right In There.

I told him she had me taped hand-to-foot and was holding a scalpel to my neck, but he didn't hear me; or maybe he didn't like what he'd heard, because he knocked again.

"Fine, *fine*," I called. "Keep your pants on."

I slid from the table and helped Phuong down, and that look of mistrust crept back into her eyes. This was it, she was probably thinking: The Big It.

I looked down at her, and I felt like shit. What was this kid to me? Just another gook. I'd assumed she was a whore, and maybe she was. Maybe she was prowling around out there in the dark, planting explosives. Maybe she was going to blow the compound sky-high. Maybe, if I were her, I'd do it myself.

But what I saw was a frightened young woman in black pajamas. Someone who had, in her brief life, been in love; someone who'd had three kids, or would have three kids but, whatever the case, now had only one and loved the hell out of it. I wanted to talk to her, to say I understood...

But, of course, I couldn't. And what the hell did I know of her life? What the hell could *I* understand?

In a couple of seconds, I'd be handing her over to Mutt and Jeff out there. They didn't look like monsters; they probably weren't. But there would be monsters aplenty in her life. The war would see to that.

I was going home in 23 hours and three minutes. It wasn't my problem.

No, my problem was, I was getting soft. I wanted to keep this kid out of jail, at least on my watch. So I decided: what the hell, why not make the last thing I did in this wretched, bug-infested room a humane act, however misguided.

I reached down and twisted her waistband. And she looked at me with a wounded dignity that surprised me, precisely because it *didn't* surprise me. What human being wants to be messed with? She reached for the elastic, to right it, and I stopped her. I pointed to the door and shook my head, and I ruffled her hair a little. She looked puzzled. Then she lowered the hand, that beautiful Psychic Hand, that she'd raised to smooth it. I smiled, and slowly, like dawn breaking over stone, her face softened.

"By Jove, she's *got* it!" I said. I hummed a bar of *The Rain in Spain* while I rumpled her collar.

She grinned; I frowned pointedly, and she took a breath and carefully wiped her face of its lovely smile.

And I opened the door.

Minelli and McArthur stood up like proper gentlemen when we came out. "Here she is," I announced. "Miss Viet Nam."

The sergeant gave Phuong the eye; she flicked me a disgusted look. It was all I could do to keep from laughing.

"You searched her?" he said.

"Every little nook and cranny," I lied. "She's clean," I told them. "Well, maybe not *clean*, but she doesn't have any weapons up her ass." I watched with glee as Pvt. McArthur's long face turned five shades of scarlet.

I told them Phuong had a baby waiting for her at home, and that they might want to send her back before it woke up. We didn't want the Good Guys to look bad, did we?

Minelli told me that was up to the captain.

"I'm too short to give a shit," I said. "But call it women's intuition, I really don't think she's Uncle Ho's right-hand man."

As he ushered his little family out the door, Minelli said he hoped that I was right.

So do I, Sergeant, I told myself. I looked at my hands. They were shaking, so I poured a quarter-cup of whiskey, lit another cigarette and filled my lungs with the marvelous, deadly smoke.

So the fuck do I.

What Dreams May Come

H. Persey Jewett III bent over his anesthesia machine and tested the connection to the first oxygen tank. His shoulders ached, and his face felt tight with fatigue; this would be his fourth patient since the run began at 0530, roughly five hours ago. Bad patients, even for Viet Nam: limbs blown off, faces gone, bellies full of frags. The last one had been a bleeder—heart hole, femoral artery ripped to shit; poor sonovabitch, black kid from Missouri, had left with one leg and stitches tracking all the way down his chest. Wonder was that he didn't leave in a bag.

It was that kind of day. The Operating Room was running full-tilt. Literally running. Techs ran into the rooms with patients and out of the rooms with empty gurneys, then reversed the procedure. Docs ran from room to room, scrubbing in where they were needed to help the primary surgeons. Nurses ran back and forth through the open corridor that bordered the suite, their arms loaded with jumbo train-wreck bandage packs grabbed from the sterile supply rack at the rear. Everybody ran around with mops and pails, swabbing tables and floors, cleaning them up so they could get gory again with the next spate of mangled bodies.

And anesthetists ran the gas, non-stop, pausing only long enough to get one patient awake and stable before they took on the next. Jewett pulled out his oversized blue kerchief, one of a dozen he'd gotten at Christmas from his wife back home in Maryland, and mopped the sweat from his face. He snapped the front of his machine closed, stood and stretched his back, cracked his aching knuckles, then double-checked the medicines in his syringes. On the radio that was

234

duct-taped high up in the corner of the room, Peter, Paul & Mary sang, *I'm leavin' on a jet plane; don't know when I'll be back again—*

"'Oh, babe, I hate to go,'" Jewett finished in a nasal and slightly out-of-tune tenor. He tapped his foot. Waiting.

Jerry Cavendish and Seth Obermeyer rolled the cart in quickly, jostling the compact form beneath its blue sheet like a load of dead meat. *Fuck*, thought Jewett. *Not another gook kid.* He reached for the chart beneath the gurney pad, glancing at the patient's face as his hand brushed past it.

It wasn't a kid. But it was, indeed, a gook. He scanned the chart quickly, then looked up sharply at Obermeyer, who was positioning himself at the patient's feet.

"What the hell's *this*?" said H. Persey Jewett III.

"Give us a hand here, won't you, Pers?" Obermeyer nodded toward the patient's head. "He's short, but he ain't no lightweight."

Jewett glared at the two techs, then at the unconscious patient. "What the fuck are we doing with this guy?"

"Well, presumably, sir," said Cavendish, "We're going to take some metal out of his abdomen. If you get hold of his head here."

Jewett grabbed the man's head and moved it, none too gently, as the two techs scooted the rest of the body onto the table. He slapped his stethoscope onto the man's bare upper chest and taped it down. "Why bother?" he said, slipping the blood pressure cuff over the patient's limp arm.

Cavendish hung the IV bottle next to Jewett then stood back, hands on hips, and watched the anesthetist clamp the gas mask over the man's face. With this, the patient stiffened; his eyes flew open, then closed again. "Presumably because of the Geneva Convention, Capitan," said Jerry Cavendish.

Jewett turned the oxygen on. "Bunch of fucking liberals," he growled.

The nurse (Alice Allen again—she of the pert black face and

firm, generous ass—for the third time today) had just opened the sterile table when Dr. Harry Conroy walked in, big hands in the air. "Well, well. Alice. Pers. We meet again. I hear this is an easy one."

Jewett glanced up briefly, his hand slowly squeezing the bag that dangled from his machine. Squeezing breath, life, oxygen and nitrous oxide into the inert form in front of him. Conroy was a decent general surgeon, in his estimation—not great, by any means, but Close Enough for Government Work, as the saying went. But Jewett didn't much like the guy. For one thing, he was married, and acted it. That wasn't natural for a man; one whole year away, you needed somebody. Jewett himself wrote faithfully, every day, to his own very lovely wife, but he spent a fair bit of quality sack time with LaCroix from the Recovery Room. Sooner or later, that's what happened with the other married guys, too. A man had certain needs. But not Conroy. Not after eight months, even—and he seemed so fucking proud of it. In his heart of hearts, Jewett suspected that Conroy couldn't get it up, or—worse yet—that he might even be a closet homo. And that, naturally enough, colored his estimation of the man.

Another thing was, Conroy was a fucking liberal.

Ordinarily, Jewett could live with their differences. Live and let live; you didn't do that in 'Nam, you wouldn't get anything done. This morning, however, they'd worked together on the last case—the black bleeder, the case that lasted two and one-half hours—and the guy's un-fucking-failing righteous prissy-ness had already rubbed Jewett's fatigued brain raw.

Conroy's eyes, bulgy and slightly walled above the blue mask, sought his; Jewett gave him a perfunctory nod and bent back to his patient. *Hope to god,* he thought, pushing a paralyzing dose of curare into the gook's vein, *that this is the last time I see your ugly puss today. Or maybe forever.*

Conroy dug a big mitt into the glove that Cavendish, already dressed in sterile gear, stretched open for him. He cleared his throat. "So. Our boy's NVA, huh?"

Jewett clenched his teeth and checked his nitrous level.

"So saith the chart," said Cavendish.

"Yeah," said Alice Allen, opening a pack of sponges onto the back table. "Would you believe it? This is one strange run. Down in One, Crawford says they got some guy they've tagged an 'Out of Country something-or-other.' Looks like a Montagnard, but he don't speak Vietnamese."

"I'll bet you five he's Cambodian," said Cavendish. "I had one of those mystery men my first case." He helped Obermeyer into his gloves. "I say, 'If they looks like a Cambodian, an' they smells like a Cambodian–'"

"Thank you, Jerry," said Obermeyer, flexing his latex-covered hands. "I'll do the same for you some day."

"Don't mention it, Hombre."

"So why don't they just call him a Cambodian, if he's a Cambodian?" said Allen wearily, stretching on her tip-toes behind Conroy to tie the top laces of the surgeon's gown.

"Because," said Cavendish. "Haven't you heard? We are not officially *in* Cambodia."

Jewett glanced down at the gook, and repressed the urge to spit into one of his taped-shut eyes. "It's about time," he said.

Conroy turned toward him. "I beg your pardon?"

"It's about time we went in there, bombed the shit out of 'em. It's where they're all coming from," said Jewett, squeezing methodically on the bag. "Hit 'em where they live. What the hell are we *here* for, anyway?"

"'They' are North Vietnamese," said the surgeon evenly, as he and the techs laid the top drapes over the patient. "Ergo, they don't 'live' in Cambodia."

Jewett narrowed his eyes. *You know fucking well what I mean.* "Tell me they aren't using the Ho Chi Minh Trail as a supply line," he said. "Tell me it doesn't go right down through Cambodia. Right through the fucking Parrot's Beak."

237

"Scalpel," said Conroy. "I didn't say that it doesn't, Pers. However, there are also civilians in Cambodia. Doesn't it make you a bit nervous to know that we're bombing indiscriminately where there are civilians who are—clamp, thank you, Jerry—who are not involved in this war?"

"Whatever it takes," said Jewett. He noted that the blood pressure was steady, picked up the syringe of morphine.

Then he set it back down, unused. *Fuck you*, he told the gook mentally. "I suppose," he said, his voice carefully bland, "you think it's fair that we have to take our precious time, when we could be working on *our* guys, to patch this little bastard up? When the whole object of this whole fucking war is to kill him?"

"I need a little more relaxation here," said the surgeon. "He's a little tight."

Jewett pushed in a bit more of the curare. Arrow poison, that's curare; some pigmy blow-pipes it into his enemy's skin, and it paralyzes him to death. Jewett toyed briefly with the idea of giving the gook more—twice, three times as much. And then just *forgetting* to squeeze the bag for a few minutes. Look, mom: no air. Little fucker couldn't raise a finger to help himself. Heh. Kill him a gook, like a proper patriot. But sure as hell, somebody'd find him out; be like that My Lai thing everybody was pissing and moaning about back home right now. *Oh, my, my, the bad soldiers killed old Papa-san!* Jewett snorted into his mask. *As if there were innocent bystanders in any of those damned villages.*

On the radio, Country Joe jangled out the *Feel Like I'm Fixin' to Die Rag.* Catchy tune, thought Jewett; but why did AFVN radio—*Armed Forces Viet Nam Radio*, mind you—play stuff by peacenik pinkos? What about the Morale of the Fucking Troops? Screw Country Joe and the Fish he rode in on; Jewett sure as shit didn't have to ask what we were fighting for.

"Look, Pers. I'm here to save lives. Clamp; now sponge right there. Good, Jerry. That's it. I don't agree with *any* part of this war, our side or theirs."

"Now, now, boys," said Alice of the Magnificent Ass, her strong black hands pulling open a sponge pack. "It's been too long a morning for a debate over politics."

"Roger *that*," said Obermeyer, stepping up onto a stool next to the surgeon. "I promise I'll try not to fall asleep in the wound, Doc."

"Good. Hold onto this, won't you? Besides," said Conroy, "this guy's probably some big Kahuna in their army. Maybe he's a general; we don't know. Seth, grab that big retractor, too—yeah, that one—and jump right on in here. Good man. Pull it out a bit more—that's it. Could damned well be that what he has to tell us might save whole platoons of our guys."

Allen stepped up to the surgeon and mopped his face with a towel, carefully avoiding the table and his sterile gown.

"Thanks, Alice," said Conroy.

Jewett clamped his jaw tightly and squeezed the air bag. He took his left hand off the carotid pulse and rested it lightly on the handle of the halothane vaporizer.

Above the belly, Conroy was pulling intestines out onto the sheets, carefully inching his fingers down the coils, mashing big fingertips into the fascia. "Well!" The surgeon stuck out his hand, and Cavendish slapped a pair of forceps into it. He smiled behind the mask, bulgy eyes suddenly merry. "As the urologist says, 'Urethra—I've found it!'"

Obermeyer chuckled behind his mask.

Jewett sighed heavily. When you'd heard a bad joke a half-dozen times, it still wasn't funny. He touched the patient's neck again, and his finger registered a quickening of the gook's—the *enemy's*—pulse. Once again, he reached toward the halothane.

Then he stopped short.

Conroy dropped a small metal fragment into a metal emesis basin. *Ping-ping.*

Jewett held his breath. He couldn't kill the gook, no. But he could make damned well sure the little fucker knew where he was, and who was who in this man's war. Quietly, he pushed in bit more curare. He reached for the nitrous knob and slowly–

–slowly–

–turned it.

Off.

On the radio, The Vanilla Fudge sang about their baby sending them a letter–a good one, not a Dear John like Harley Hooper got the other day. Damn, now, that was harsh. Jewett hummed along tunelessly, squeezing the ventilator bag in rhythm. *Lucky I'm still giving you oxygen, baby*, he mentally told the gook.

Above the patient, Conroy dropped a few more small metal fragments into his basin. *Ping-ping*. At his side, Obermeyer held the incision open with retractors. Across from them, Cavendish leaned against the Mayo stand and doled out clamps. In the corner of the room, Alice Allen bent over, her magnificent ass to Jewett, and arranged bloody sponges in carefully counted piles. The Fudge demanded a ticket for an aero-plane. Jewett grinned tightly behind his mask, tapped his foot to the music.

Hot damn, he felt good. He felt better than he'd felt since this God-blasted day had begun.

Below him, the gook's eyes began to water beneath their white tape strips, and small beads of sweat stood out on his brown forehead.

Jewett nodded to the music.

"Here you are, Alice." Above the patient, the surgeon handed a shattered spleen off into the nurse's basin. "Pers, how's his BP?"

Jewett pumped up the blood pressure cuff, let it down. "Textbook," he said, beaming innocently at Conroy behind his mask, which had slipped down beneath his nose. "One-twenty over eighty." In truth, it was 165 over 100 and rising. The carotid artery throbbed violently beneath his fingers; the gook's pulse was hovering at 110. *That would be the pain*, thought Jewett with great satisfaction. And, perhaps, the panic. *Yep, we're feeling pretty fucking desperate, aren't we, Charlie? All awake and aware in there, with that pompous mother snip-snip-snipping away at us, and hey—all we can do about it is sweat and cry.* Brilliant twist, that it should be Save-the-Gooks-Conroy who doled out the pain. *Ah, irony! Snip. Snip. Snip.*

The Jefferson Airplane wailed from the radio, and Jewett hummed along with Gracie's admonition to feed his head.

Conroy's slightly walled eyes focused on the anesthetist for a moment, as if he had something important to say. Jewett steeled himself and returned a steady gaze. At length, the surgeon looked back down into the wound. Cavendish handed him a clamp, which he applied to a small but persistent bleeder.

"Look at that baby shoot," said Cavendish.

"Hmm," said Conroy.

Allen held another sponge count, pulling the bloody bits of gauze apart on a sheet with a long metal forceps. Obermeyer stepped down and counted the sterile squares on the back table.

Closing time, folks. Jewett pumped up the cuff once more and watched the mercury bob at the 175 mark. He pressed lightly on the carotid artery. 120. Still squeezing the black air bag with his right hand, he picked up a syringe full of neostigmine in his left. He watched Conroy stitch the muscle. Almost time to reverse the curare's paralysis. This could be sticky; as much as he'd love the gook to come screaming off the table before he was closed up, he didn't think Conroy would go for it. He balanced the syringe in his hand and waited.

"Is he a little light?"

Jewett looked up. "You're almost done, right?" He raised an eyebrow. "I'm lightening him up, of course. Why do you ask?"

Conroy straightened his back and rolled his shoulders. "I don't know. Just a feeling. He seems...I don't know—"

Jewett looked him in the eye again. "It would be pretty stupid to put him any more under if you're almost done."

"Can't you give him a little...I don't know, maybe a little morphine or something?"

241

Jewett stared at him. Hard. Stared those wall-ish eyes into a vague uncertainty. "He's had enough," he told the surgeon.

Cavendish handed Conroy another suture, and the surgeon dug the needle into the last bit of muscle. *So there, shithead,* thought Jewett with a giddy rush of glee. *Not a damned thing you can do about it, is there?*

He injected the neostigmine when Conroy was half-done with the skin sutures. A little later than usual. It would take the medicine five or ten minutes to kill the paralysis, but since the curare was the only thing keeping the gook on the table, he figured it might not be a bad thing for the fucker to wake up after the doc had left the room. You could only push this thing so far with a goody-goody like Conroy. He discreetly, left-handedly, wiped the gook's face with a towel and pressed the tape on his left eye back down where the still-streaming tears had detached it.

"Is this the last patient?" said Obermeyer, who had stripped off his gown and was dumping saline into a sterile basin.

Cavendish dipped a sponge into the liquid and cleaned off the incision. "Presumably," he said.

Conroy set a pile of fluffy dressings over the stitches and looked hard at Jewett. "A little late, aren't we?"

"Beg pardon?"

"You've usually got him squirming by the last stitch. Off your mark?"

"Long day." Jewett continued to bag the patient. "Weren't you just yanking my chain about how light he was? Can't have it both ways."

Over the surgeon's shoulder, Simon and Garfunkel crooned about feeling groovy.

Conroy pulled his gloves off, still watching the anesthetist. Jewett sat nonchalantly, left hand on the patient's pulse, right hand squeezing, squeezing, squeezing. Obermeyer was gathering up the instruments, and Alice Allen had brought in the mop.

Cavendish rattled an empty gurney into the room. "Your chariot awaits."

"Ready in moments," said Jewett. From the radio came the first wailing chords of *Green, Green Grass of Home*. "Man, Jerry," said Jewett, as he watched the patient's abdomen rise and fall, "Don't I just love that song." He sang softly, in his nasal, slightly off-key tenor, "'The hometown looks the same—'"

Conroy's gaze faltered, and he dropped his gloves in the trash. The surgeon sighed heavily. Then he turned his back and walked out.

Commendation

The Lieutenant stuck her head out of her room.

Alice Allen held up the phone receiver. "It's for you."

The voice on the other end was nasal and chipper. "How's my favorite officer?"

The Lieutenant smiled. Scully. God, it'd been a month since she'd heard from him. "I'm short, Scully. Really short. Three more days. Other than that, I'm depressed as hell. How the hell are *you*?"

"You know me, I keep on keeping on. I got five more months to go in this shithole; I'm the one should be depressed as hell."

The Lieutenant snorted into the receiver. "Serves you right: you're the one who re-upped. Anybody who signs up for another year in this place is obviously certifiable."

"Couldn't pass up the chance of being worshipped and feared for a whole 'nother year. But enough about the gods. What's biting your ass?"

She drummed her fingernails on the receiver. "I had my 'Hail and Farewell' last night, and guess what?"

"What?"

The Lieutenant sighed. "Look, you know me. None of this stuff really means jack shit to me. None of the praises, awards, whatever. Right? Still—"

"No bronze star."

"—I didn't get—" She stopped suddenly, and pulled the phone from her ear, gave it a *look*, returned it. "How'd you know?"

He chuckled. "Ah, Lieutenant, do you forget who you're talking to? *I got the ways and the means.*"

She sat down heavily at the table. It was the kitchenette of the hooch, and the black telephone sat on the round wooden tabletop, surrounded by well-thumbed and damply sticky magazines from months past. The Lieutenant picked up a coverless copy of Time and idly turned the pages. She noted that four of the Chicago Seven had been jailed for Contempt, and that an oil slick was spreading over Tampa Bay. "Silly me," she said. "How could I forget." She leaned on her elbows over the magazine, the receiver to her mouth. "It's nothing, really. I mean, hey, everybody here gets a bronze star. They pass them out to the guys who clean the latrines. It's just that, well—" she turned a page—"they pass them out to the guys who clean the latrines. I've been working my butt off for twelve months, and—"

"I can tell you why, if you really want to know." Scully's voice had that irritating I-know-a-secret quality that had always set her teeth on edge when they were stationed together, first at Phu Bai and then at Chu Lai.

She turned another page. "You'll tell me, whether I want to know or not."

"Of course," he crowed. "What good is it, being privy to all this stuff if you can't pass it along?"

"Well, then, do what you must."

"Ah, I just love me a submissive woman." There was a sound of shuffling papers on the other end of the line. "Let's see," he mused. "Why, here it is: a note from your superior officer, the esteemed Head Nurse at Chu Lai's own 27th Surg. Former head nurse—she's been gone a month. Ready?"

The Lieutenant shook her head. Ah, Scully. Nineteen months in Viet Nam, and the little weasel hadn't changed a whit. "Go for it," she said.

"This is your personnel file I'm looking at, mind you, a copy of the salient pages forwarded to me by my own very good Mafia connection Horowitz."

She turned another page in *Time*: "Midnight Cowboy" was nominated for a Best Picture Oscar. She tossed the magazine aside—the damned thing was three months old. "Scully, that's horribly unethical." She paused for effect, then added, "So what's it say?"

"It's just a little old memo from our mutual friend the Light Colonel, to the effect that you're not to be given any extraordinary awards for service due to...let's see...'deliberate and repeated flaunting of hospital regulations.'"

The Lieutenant clenched her teeth. "That's 'flouting.' The woman's not only an ass, she's doesn't know her grammar. Christ, that's disgusting. Scully, that's just so un-fucking-fair." She thought a moment. "Does she say exactly how I've 'flaunted' these hypothetical hospital regs?"

"I told you it was just a little memo. No details, I'm afraid. If it's any consolation, Sweetie, I think you done a great job, getting through this year."

The Lieutenant stared at the table, her mood black. "Yeah, well, all you saw was my warm-up. I saved my best 'flaunting' for this place."

"Seriously, I think you're a real peach, and I'm proud to have had the opportunity to pry into your paperwork."

"Thanks, Scully. You're a mensch." The Lieutenant took off her glasses and set them on the tabletop. She closed her eyes. She was beginning to get a headache, and she wanted a drink. She felt humiliated. And thoroughly pissed. The *balls* of the Lieutenant-Colonel, attaching a sniveling little memo to her personnel file, making her look like a fool. She'd spent her life in the O.R. for the past year, blood up to her ears, slogging through twelve- to twenty-four-hour shifts six days a week, side-by-side with her peers. And now, when she was about to leave, she was the only nurse at the 12th who supposedly didn't deserve a Bronze Star. Probably the only nurse in the whole damned Army.

The phone crackled at her ear. "Seriously. Just think about it: a whole year. And you have survived. You have *persevered*!" He paused dramatically. "Frankly, My Dear, you deserve a real hand for that."

"Thanks, Scully," she said.

"No. I mean it. From my bottom to my heart. You deserve a great big hand."

The Lieutenant sat down at the bar in the Officer's Club, her mind churning with consternation.

Two stools down, Pers Jewett glanced up at her. "Well, well. I can hardly see you over this bar, Honey Buns," said the anesthetist. "You're so Short."

The bartender handed her a gin-and-tonic. "On the house, Lieutenant," he said, wiping his hands on the front of his dirty apron.

"Thanks, Harvey." The Lieutenant nodded to Jewett and stared glumly at her drink.

She felt someone sit down beside her and glanced up to see Sarah Dinsmore raising a half-consumed glass of chardonnay. "Heeeey—somebody's about to go back to the World," said Sarah. "God, that must feel great. I've got four months before I catch that Freedom Bird, and I'm just so damned jealous. Cheers, Honey." She took a sip and tapped the Lieutenant's glass. "Next one's on me."

The Lieutenant sighed. "Sure. Why not."

"Tsk, tsk, tsk." Sarah gave her a searching glance. "If we're going home, why are we so icky?"

The Lieutenant turned on her stool to face her. "Sarah, do you think I do a good job? I mean, *did* a good job? I guess I'm in the past tense now."

Sarah pulled back. "Whoa, heavy. What—you mean, in the O.R.?"

"Well, yes. I guess. And in general."

"In general? As in, do you want me to evaluate your life?" She sat up primly on the stool. "I don't feel quite...qualified to make that judgment, Ma'am."

"Was I good enough," said the Lieutenant, "to get a Bronze Star?"

Sarah nodded sagely. "Aha. I think we've come to the heart of the matter." She patted the Lieutenant's arm. "Of course you were, Honey. Who the hell isn't? They give them out like lollipops at Halloween." She pulled a quarter from her pocket and set it on the back of her hand. Working her knuckles slightly, she made the coin walk from her pinky to her thumb. Then it fell off.

"You're getting better."

Sarah re-set the coin. "Four more months to practice. I get out, I'll tour the magic circuit. Sooo. Why didn't they give you your medal? Do you know? Or should I not ask."

The Lieutenant hunched over her drink. "Because I don't wear my combat boots when I dance. Because I dated an EM."

"Really? Who told you that?"

"A clerk from the 27th. He says my old commanding officer put a note on my record."

Sarah whistled. "She actually said it was because of the combat boots?"

"No. But that's what she meant."

"Harvey, fill up this very short person's glass," said Sarah. "Wow. A clerk told you that." She tipped her hand, and the quarter again set off across her knuckles.

The Lieutenant watched the coin drop to the bar. The bartender set out another gin-and-tonic and removed her empty glass.

"Well, then." Sarah stuck the quarter back into her pocket. "It must be true."

"I guess." The Lieutenant took a gulp of her drink. "He didn't think it was fair, either. He said he thought I deserved a big hand for making it through all the bullshit."

"He's right."

"There were a lot of nurses who did a lot worse things than I ever did," said the Lieutenant. "There was a Major who kept a monkey as a pet. In Chu Lai. The Lieutenant-Colonel never said a thing to her about it. And I'm sure there's something in the regulations that *that* violates."

"Possibly. But a Major's pretty high on the food chain. Lieutenants," said Sarah, "are expendable."

"I suppose." The Lieutenant took another gulp of the gin-and-tonic. "But other nurses dated EMs, too. Hell, a friend of mine claimed she deflowered the Chaplain's Assistant on the chapel altar, for Chrissake!"

"Hmmm." Sarah shrugged. "Maybe she was jealous."

"Jealous of what?"

"I don't know. Your youth?" Sarah leaned close. "Maybe this Light Colonel of yours had a crush on you."

The Lieutenant shivered. "God, I hope not. What a thought." She stirred the remnants of her drink with her index finger; the ice had melted completely. "If I *did* swing that way, I should hope I'd have better taste."

The two sat in silence for a moment, listening to Janis Joplin sing *Turtle Blues* on the tape recorder behind the bar. Then Sarah said, "You know, it could be your attitude."

The Lieutenant looked up at her. "What attitude?"

"Well... You're not exactly a patriot, you know. I mean, most of us—take Sandy, for instance, or even Alice—we tend to find some redeeming...*thing*...to being here. Some girls even *like* it. Like Di Di, she did. And why not? It's *real* nursing. And all these men... But you—I don't know—" She rested her elbow on the bar and assessed the Lieutenant. "Do you really want to talk about this? I mean, it's not as if we've been friends our whole lives, exactly—"

The Lieutenant shrugged. "Sure. Go for it."

"Well, it's like—" She paused, swirling the last of her wine in her glass. "It's like you take this war personally."

The Lieutenant stiffened. "It's sucked up a year of my life; I consider that pretty personal."

"I rest my case." Sarah drained her glass. "It's not that I'm exactly gung-ho about it, myself," she added, "But the fact of the matter

249

is, I wouldn't be here if I hadn't signed up. And that's the same with you, too. So the assumption is, we all had some reason to be here–"

"I was young. Naive. Stupid."

"We all were. I'm sure there wasn't any one of us realized what we were getting into. But even those of us who have doubts, well, we're not so–I don't know–*vocal*, maybe? Or unhappy? I mean, we are serving our country." She patted the Lieutenant's arm again. "Look, all I'm saying is, we're not the experts. What do we know about the motives behind all this? So...the way I see it, most of us just kind of stay in the middle; we don't go out and march for either side. We just do what we have to, to keep ourselves busy until it's time to leave." She glanced across the Lieutenant to where H. Persey Jewett III sat. "Whaddya think, Pers? Am I right?"

The anesthetist gave the Lieutenant a haughty look. "You don't really want my opinion," he told her flatly.

"No," said the Lieutenant. "I'm sure I don't."

Jewett rose and laid an MPC bill on the bar. "I would like to say, however: for a commie, you've got great legs." He threw her a mock salute and walked off.

Sarah picked up her new glass of wine. "As I said, most of us stay in the middle," she said.

The Lieutenant fished the piece of lime from her drink and squeezed it into the glass. "What about Cesak? You can't say she didn't have an attitude problem. But nobody held it against her. And she–"

"Got her Bronze Star. Sure. But she was funnier about it. It's like, she could laugh at herself. No offense, but you're pretty intense about it all. That puts some people off. Brass, especially. No offense." She sipped her wine, then lifted her glass in a salute. "But still, you should have gotten your Bronze Star. Even if you didn't believe in any of this, you worked as hard as everybody who did."

"Thanks." said the Lieutenant. "I guess."

The Lieutenant was packing her tape reels into her footlocker when she heard a knock at her door.

"There's a guy out front with a package for you," said Allen. "He said to tell you it's a gift from some clerk up in Chu Lai."

The Lieutenant walked the length of the hooch to the front door, where she found a large man in a warrant officer's uniform. He was holding a package. It was wrapped in a page from the *Stars and Stripes* and tied with a rather ratty pink ribbon. "Gift from Spec 5 Scully," he said, handing it to her.

She hefted the parcel; whatever lay beneath the paper felt firm and irregularly shaped. "Did he give you a message to go with it?" she asked the man.

"He said it had something to do with his phone call. Something about appreciation for your efforts, whatever that means."

The Lieutenant thanked him and brought the gift back to the table, where Allen was writing a letter. She set it down and pulled at the ribbon. Allen glanced over. "Oh! Present from an admirer?"

"An old friend," said the Lieutenant, tearing the tape that held the newsprint together. "I can't imagine what—"

The paper fell away. The Lieutenant's jaw dropped.

Then she began to laugh.

Allen stood to get a view of the gift. Her eyes grew enormous in her dark face. "Oh, lord," she said. "That's...Is that really what I think it is?"

"Oh, yes—" the Lieutenant gasped. "Ab—solutely."

Allen gave her a look of horror. "And that's *funny*? Girl, you are insane."

The Lieutenant collapsed into the chair, tears running down her cheeks.

A door opened behind them; DiDi Britten stepped out of her room. "What's going on?" she asked.

Allen lifted the plastic bag gingerly with two fingers and held it up. The object inside shifted, leaving a pinkish liquid smear. Britten moved to the table for a closer look. She covered her mouth with her hands. "Oh, geez! It's not—*human*, is it?"

"I'd say so," said Allen. "Note the opposable thumb: ain't too many other species that got 'em."

Britten looked from the bag to Allen. "What on earth is that about?"

"Ask her," said Allen, nodding toward the Lieutenant, who was still giggling fitfully, polishing the lenses of her glasses with her shirt. "Me, I don't traffic in spare parts."

The Lieutenant tried to pull herself together. "S-s-somebody's finally given me a—" She began to laugh again, bit her tongue—"a *hand* for my performance in Viet Nam."